C000050410

Stand Against
INJUSTICE

Michelle Diskin Bates

malcolm down
PUBLISHING

First published 2018 by Malcolm Down Publishing Ltd.
www.malcolmdown.co.uk

British Library Cataloguing in Publication Data
A catalogue record for this book is available from the British Library.

ISBN 978-1-910786-24-6

Cover design by Esther Kotecha
Art direction by Sarah Grace
Back cover photograph by Paul Mockford

Printed in the UK by Bell & Bain Ltd, Glasgow

This book is dedicated to the ones I love:

To three extraordinary people, my beloved children Carine, Shane and Emma Jane. Throughout this long and unenviable journey you were my anchor, keeping my feet firmly on the ground. Your love and your generosity of spirit helped keep me sane.

Also to my kind, loving and patient husband, Peter, my best friend and constant supporter. At least I have one fan!

And to Barry, always my little brother.

Contents

Acknowledgements

Can I ever truly thank you, my darling Peter? You have always believed in me and in this book, even when I lost faith in my own ability to impart this difficult story. You cooked meals for me when I could hardly lift my head from the computer. You put a curfew on my work time because I needed to sleep, too. Encouraged me even when you felt totally frustrated with the whole process. You also loved and supported me as I 'killed my darlings' during the editing process. Your unconditional love gave me strength, I couldn't have done this without you.

Thanks also to Richard Herkes, my early-days Editorial Consultant. I am so grateful for the edits and direction you gave me for the manuscript, and for believing I could do this.

Of course, huge thanks to Malcolm Down and Sarah Grace Publishing. Malcolm and Sarah, from the very start you believed in this book, even when others said 'no, this is not for us', or 'this story is dead, there's no interest in it anymore'. You stuck with me even in the dry desert moments, and when life had to take precedence over writing. I'm grateful for the extensions to the publication date, it meant so much to know you believed in me as a writer and author before I was one. And dear Chloe, editing can be such a painful process. Thank you for ploughing through my book and putting manners on it: my structure, grammar and punctuation needed urgent medical attention. You also helped me to find an ending for the book even though our battle for justice continues to this day.

And lastly to our dear friend Robin Croxon, you always believed this was a story that should be heard. You encouraged me with my writing even when my 'manuscript' was little more than a bundle of disjointed and pain filled essays. Your knowledge of the world of publishing was invaluable, and without your help I would still be searching through lists of publishers, not knowing which way to turn. Thank you for being there from the start.

Foreword

This book is, simultaneously, most disturbing yet uplifting and inspirational. In forensic detail, it interweaves an anatomy of the high-profile wrongful conviction and imprisonment of Barry George for the murder of Jill Dando, the much-loved journalist and television presenter, with the author's stand with, and for, her brother in a fight for truth and justice, and against all of the forces of the State that were marshalled towards obtaining a conviction, and holding onto it, with little or no regard as to whether Barry George was the actual murderer or not.

In terms of the comprehensive chronology of Barry George's wrongful conviction, it provides a rare insight into the workings of the criminal justice system that lays bare how its operating notion of "justice" jars with the widely held belief (myth) that the core function of the criminal justice system is to protect the public from the harm of acts labelled crime, by convicting the factually guilty (i.e. those who actually committed the offence), whilst guarding against the wrongful conviction of the factually innocent (i.e. ensuring that those who did not commit the offence are not convicted).

Indeed, a common theme of miscarriage of justice cases is that the police and prosecution often operate within a paradigm of "tunnel vision", which sees them identify a potential suspect first, and then work inwards to build a case against them rather than working from the evidence out in criminal investigations. At such times, rather than a genuine concern with trying to apprehend those who commit alleged criminal offences, the criminal justice system is better understood as a machinery that works, instead, to convert forms of information that may have no direct bearing on the alleged offence in the manufacture of forms of "evidence" deemed fit for the requirements of the judicial process, i.e. have a greater probability than not of obtaining a conviction.

I use inverted commas for evidence here as the forms of "evidence" that are constructed for use in criminal trials, and accepted as admissible by the courts, are inherently unreliable, yet the judicial system is designed to regard them to be sufficient to convict individuals who may be, or are in fact, innocent. It is in this sense that the book highlights that to understand the ease with which innocent victims can be, and are, wrongly convicted, there is a need, first, to distinguish between criminal justice system forms of "evidence" and evidence as truth, with the latter being the only legitimate basis upon which convictions should be obtained.

As this bears on the Barry George case, various forms of relatively innocuous information were combined and presented at his trial as "evidence" that he may have, or did indeed, murder Jill Dando. This included alleged eyewitness accounts, which conflicted in terms of timings and places, that claimed to see Mr George in the vicinity on the day of the murder when his presence in the area was to be expected as he lived locally. Eight photos and stories about Jill Dando that had been cut out of approximately 800 old newspapers and magazines found in Mr George's apartment by police officers, that were presented to the press and the public as though he had cut them out himself, presumably in an attempt to prove he had an obsession with Ms Dando and to establish a possible motive. One wonders how many photos or stories might have been culled from those newspapers and magazines in the late 1990s about Victoria Beckham, Julia Roberts or Britney Spears (or any other major public figure of the time), for instance? But, they were not who the police were seeking to establish a link with. And a single particle of Firearms Discharge Residue (FDR), which his successful appeal accepted had no probative value at all, and which was likely a product of contamination in the forensic science lab, that was claimed to match the FDR found at the crime scene. In and of themselves, it is unlikely that any of these things would be enough to even charge, let alone convict, Barry George. Taken together, however, they apparently demolished his presumed innocence status in the eyes of the jury who duly found him guilty.

The obvious consequence of this is that the criminal justice system fails both victims of miscarriages of justice and their families, and the victims of crime and their families, too, when the wrong person is convicted for a crime that they did not commit and the guilty escape justice with the potential and reality of committing further crimes whilst they enjoy their wrongful liberty. Crucially, this failure carries with it an extensive array of harms that can and does split families apart, ruin reputations and cause profound forms of social, psychological, physical and financial harm that can have on-going and often permanent effects on all aspects of primary and secondary victim's lives.

Barry George's case is not unique in this regard, as such miscarriages of justice are neither rare nor exceptional occurrences. Readers may be aware of other notorious cases such as those of the Guildford Four or the Birmingham Six that rocked the British justice system to its core. The problem is a system that is designed to work on the basis that the decisions of the courts are correct and to protect against the overturning of convictions, whether rightful or wrongful, rather than a concern with whether alleged innocent victims of wrongful conviction and/or imprisonment are telling the truth.

It is this aspect of the book that should disturb any notion that the so-called presumption of innocence acts to protect the innocent from being convicted for alleged crimes that they did not commit: police officers and prosecutors routinely cause such wrongful convictions in the normal course of their duties and are likely unaware that they have done anything wrong, nor of the injustices and widespread forms of harm that they cause. It is just as concerning that a decade since he overturned his conviction, Barry George, his sister and their supporters are still locked in a battle for compensation for his 8 years of wrongful imprisonment against a system that steadfastly refuses to recognise his innocence despite the

Court of Appeal quashing his conviction and a not guilty verdict being given at his subsequent retrial.

At the same time, *Stand Against Injustice* operates on an altogether different level to tell the very personal story of Michelle Diskin Bates' unequivocal and unconditional love for her vulnerable brother, who has multiple challenges and who was simply not able to stand up for himself against the onslaught from the police and prosecution who seemed hell-bent on convicting him.

For Michelle, it was a moral obligation that she could not turn away from in good conscience: she says that she knew her brother was innocent and had to stand with him no matter what it cost or what sacrifices had to be made. At the extreme, this involved being away from her three young children and husband in Ireland at vital times in their own lives to be with her brother in England, which is presented as something that she had no choice but to do as it was what God wanted her to do.

This reference to her Christian faith is something that gels well with my experience of other primary and secondary victims of wrongful conviction and imprisonment, particularly those that I have met in the United States, who seem more able to survive and move beyond the devastations that miscarriages of justice can and do inflict, and rebuild their lives in ways that those without faith seem less able to do.

This may well explain another feature of the book which sets it apart from others of the same genre. Written with great integrity and without even a hint of self-pity or hatred towards, or vengeance against, those responsible for causing her brother's wrongful conviction or who played a part in preventing its overturn or are currently refusing him compensation, Michelle has a clear focus to simply tell the truth, warts and all. Her hope is that lessons might be learnt that serve to prevent similar miscarriages of justice in the future or to act as a road map to guide those who unfortunately find themselves in a similar situation and are fighting against their own miscarriage of justice or that of a loved one.

In this regard, the book is courageous in its honesty with no sacred cows that Michelle is afraid to confront, whether that be the police, the media, Barry's own legal team or even Barry himself. As she tells her story of the Barry George case, and the pivotal part that she played, and is still playing, Michelle Diskin Bates has produced a rare and important book. *Stand Against Injustice* will, undoubtedly, make you think differently about the criminal justice system from hereon, and not in a good way. It will also show you what can be achieved when an (extra)ordinary woman on a mission from God with little or no apparent resources makes a demand for truth and justice for her brother and will not take no for an answer.

Dr Michael Naughton
Law School and School of Sociology, politics and International
Studies (SPAIS)
University of Bristol, UK
September 2018

Introduction

26th April 1999. Fulham, South West London.
A lone woman bustles along the quiet thoroughfare on her way to work. It is a grey and drizzly day. She peers out from under her black umbrella, glancing absentmindedly at the substantial two and three storey Victorian buildings that make up this respectable street she lives on. Stalwart homes, well maintained, most with an impressive price tag of over £1.5 million. It is 7:00am and most residents are still at home, their parked cars lining both sides of the street, leaving just enough room for a vehicle to squeeze through.

"That was why," she would later say, "it caught my attention. A maroon-coloured saloon car was double parked on the other side of the street, partially blocking the road. There was a man there, too, standing beside it. Probably a cabbie, he was much too shabby to be a chauffeur."

Something about him makes her look again. *What is he doing?* She takes another peek from under her umbrella. The man seems not to want to be looked at, hiding his face from her as he rubs at the raindrops on the windscreen, using his hand and leaving smears on the glass. *Surely he should be using a cloth?* Dismissing him from her mind, she passes on by and then forgets about him.

At about the same time, another occupant of this elegant avenue in Fulham emerges from the front door of her apartment. She, too, peers along the street, though her gaze is deliberate and observant. She'd always been a security conscious person and that day, because she was to carry quite a few boxes to the boot of her car, she needed to make sure the street was safe. Her task entailed moving between the house and the car with boxes in her arms and she didn't want to leave either door unlocked if it might invite opportunistic thieves. Ascertaining that there is no one else in the street, she decides it is not necessary to lock and unlock the car and the front door for every trip, making her job much simpler. She soon finishes and makes her way to work.

In another part of Fulham, a newly-married woman arrives for her first day of work at Hammersmith And Fulham Action on Disability (HAFAD), an advice centre for the disabled in the local area.

A new marriage, a new home, and now a new job, she thinks happily to herself as she rings the front doorbell. *I am so looking forward to working here.*

As was her habit, she had arrived early, 8:30am, so she could be organised for the day ahead. A chirpy cleaning lady answers the door.

"I wouldn't usually let anyone in, but I recognise you from your interview," she assures. "Come on in, I'll be finished in a few minutes. You go on and make yourself comfortable. The manager will be here soon."

Left alone in her new back room office, the new employee hangs up her coat, gets out her notepads and pens, lays them out on her desk and waits patiently for the others to arrive.

Chiswick, West London.

A newly engaged couple have recently returned from a delightful holiday abroad. Both of them have prestigious jobs: he works in a busy London hospital as a Consultant Gynaecologist, she is a much sought after and loved TV presenter with the BBC. Together they are flying high, living the dream. It will be a very busy year for both of them. They are due to be married in September and there is still so much to do – plans to be put in place, fittings to be organised for the dresses, and they both still have to go to work. But it is a happy overload, and they are looking forward to the future.

Rising from the breakfast table, the woman pulls on her classic cream-coloured mac, grabs her bag and keys from the hall table and climbs into her pale blue BMW convertible. She has some errands to run this morning, and will drive across London to her own home in Fulham before her meeting with her agent at 11:30.

Five hundred and sixty miles away as the crow flies, in Southern Ireland, another woman is reluctantly waking. "Oh no, is it really time to get up again?" I moan as I stretch and roll over. The display on the digital clock near the bed reads 7:30am, and I wish I could just snuggle down and go back to sleep. I'd already slept through my husband's departure for work at 06:15, but my three children wouldn't get themselves up and organised for school. Yes, it was time to rise and greet the day. "Come on, sleepy heads, rise and shine . . ." I sing out as I head downstairs. Their reply is an echo of my own previous groans.

Nothing could have prepared me for what was to follow. In my wildest imaginings I could not have conceived that the terrible murder of a woman in Fulham, someone I had never met, was about to alter the whole course of my family's life forever. Nor that I, and the three other women, would find ourselves embroiled in a series of high profile trials, a wrongful conviction, and a battle for justice that would continue for almost two decades.

BBC Presenter Shot Dead

"BBC television presenter Jill Dando has died after she was shot in the head on the doorstep of her home. Ms Dando, 37, who presented Crimewatch UK and Holiday, suffered a fatal brain injury in the attack in Fulham, West London.

She was taken to nearby Charing Cross Hospital, where she was confirmed dead on arrival at 1303 BST (1203 GMT).

Her post-mortem examination later revealed that she had received a single gunshot wound to the head."

(Excerpt from BBC Online, Monday, April 26, 1999 Published at 14:55 GMT 15:55 UK)

Justice is never served by the conviction of the innocent.

Michelle Diskin Bates

Psalm 27:11-14

11. Teach me your way, Lord;
    lead me in a straight path
    because of my oppressors.

12. Do not turn me over to the desire of my foes,
    for false witnesses rise up against me,
    spouting malicious accusations.

13. I remain confident of this:
    I will see the goodness of the Lord
    in the land of the living.

14. Wait for the Lord;
    be strong and take heart
    and wait for the Lord.

1

The Day the News Broke

25th May 2000

The day had begun with such promise; a beautiful springtime day. I'd already driven my husband to work and dropped my three children off at school. Housework awaited me, but I seemed to flit effortlessly from task to task as if on autopilot, bringing order to our unruly home. I wasn't really listening to the 9am news when it came on RTÉ (Raidió Teilifís Éireann) that morning. I'd only turned the radio on to wait for the Gerry Ryan Show, which was scheduled after the news. Gerry's programme wasn't always my cup of tea, but he could make me laugh out loud (or groan in utter exasperation) as he regaled his listeners with his current topic of discussion. Gerry's subject matter was often controversial, too: he could be light-hearted and flippant one moment and a hard-nosed interrogator the next, but he was a man who cared about the downtrodden, and would champion a cause with determination and compassion, which I admired. This morning I didn't have much time to listen, but I could catch a half hour or so, I thought.

It didn't feel like any ordinary day. I'd felt a tingling, an excitable frisson that I couldn't explain from the moment it had begun. There seemed to be a glow over it, as though I was seeing it through rose-tinted glasses. Everything was gleaming, pink and shiny. The smell of the lavender polish and the subtle sheen from the uncluttered surfaces gave me a great sense of achievement and satisfaction. These days, I never quite managed to get all the housework done. I always seemed to be rushing around but never actually catching up, since becoming a mature student at the Cork Institute of Technology (CIT) last year. Attending college as well as being a wife and a mother meant that time always seemed to be needed for something or someone else. Being able to attend the ladies' midweek prayer meeting was out of the ordinary, but I was going to make it today.

I had taken extra care getting dressed this morning in something other than student attire, and I had found the time to put on some make-up – another treat that I never quite found time to indulge in anymore.

Lord God, thank You for this day, for the freedom to have a few hours to myself. The sun is shining, the children are at school and the house is clean . . . Alleluia, I prayed silently as I began applying my eyeshadow.

"Police have today named the man in custody for the murder of Jill Dando . . ."

The newscaster's voice interrupted my reverie and I became vaguely attentive. *Oh good*, I mused with an absentminded detachment, smoothing pink blusher onto my cheeks. *It's about time someone was brought to justice for that awful crime. That poor family, I'm sure it's been about a year now.*

Not having lived in the UK since 1973, I hadn't really been following the case about the senseless murder of a much-loved TV presenter; it was a crime that had taken place in London and I'd felt somewhat removed from it. The case did remind me, though, of the killing of Veronica Guerin in Dublin. Also a journalist, she was killed because she had been investigating organised crime. She had been targeted before as a warning, shot in the leg on her doorstep, but had survived. Then, on 26th June 1996, she was gunned down whilst sitting in her car, which was stopped at traffic lights on the outskirts of Dublin. A gunman riding pillion on a motorcycle shot her six times, fatally injuring her, before the pair fled the scene. To me, there were parallels with the Dando case: both women worked against the criminal fraternity in a very public way, both had been attacked on their doorsteps, and both were now dead.

Of course, we couldn't help but be aware of the Dando killing, even in Ireland. Jill's lovely smiling face, the iconic image of her wearing that long red sequinned dress, her recent engagement to renowned gynaecologist Alan Farthing – all of this had been reported on news channels here, too. It seemed inconceivable that the police had not been able to find her killer yet.

"... his name is Barry Bulsara, and he lives in the Fulham area ..." the newscaster continued.

The mascara wand in my hand froze halfway to my eye. I stood there transfixed gazing into the mirror in the hallway, my mouth open and my eyes open even wider, but I was blind, seeing nothing but mist. My breath caught in my throat as tremors started to course through my body and I remember flushing hot and cold. *What just happened? I couldn't have heard that right. Say it again, oh please, say it again.* I stood rooted to the spot, willing the newsreader to repeat her words, to confirm the name that I couldn't believe I'd just heard ... *Bulsara.* That was the name my brother Barry had used when he'd given me his email address a couple of years ago, although we'd never actually written to each other.

"It's Freddy Mercury's real name," he'd explained. "He's the lead singer with Queen. They're my favourite rock band."

Go on, say it! I silently implored again, but the newscaster didn't comply. She just went on relaying today's news to the RTÉ listenership. I didn't hear another word of it.

The Gerry Ryan Show soon came on the air, but I didn't hear any of that either. My world had just shifted off its axis. My wonderful day of joy and freedom had been whisked away like a rug being pulled from under me, and I was left confused and bewildered, the taste of ashes in my mouth. I felt physically sick.

Quivering panic rushed over me and I couldn't seem to keep still. *Move,* my mind said, and I started pacing aimlessly from room to room, wringing my hands and talking to myself. *Have I just gone mad?* I felt I must have. *Things like this don't happen to people like us.* I so hoped that I had misheard, but I didn't know how to check without looking like a complete idiot.

Ring the radio station, my mind advised me, trying to find a logical solution.

Good Lord, No! my internal dialogue leapt in response. *If this really is true, you'll be alerting the media to your family, and if it proves to be nothing in the end, you'll look like a proper fool!*

Ring Mum, the logical inner voice continued.

Oh, Michelle, don't be so ridiculous. How can you ask your mother if Barry has been arrested for the murder of Jill Dando? She'll think you've lost your grip on reality.

Agitation driving me, I paced on and on . . . from the front door, along the short tiled hallway and into the kitchen. I really loved this large open plan room, which we'd had tiled with matte blue Italian floor slabs, but it brought me no joy this morning. Back out into the hall I trudged, then into the front room, only to tramp a trail back out into the hall again. Over and over I prowled, seeking some sort of sensible answer to a question that made my mind reel. As I did so, a myriad of other questions invaded my stupefied brain until I thought my head would burst.

Was this real?

What would happen to us, and to Barry?

Would this prove to be a mistake?

What about friends and family, would they need to know?

How would I tell my husband?

The anxious pacing continued back and forth, wearing tread-marks into my freshly vacuumed carpets. The rosy, cosy world I inhabited just a few moments ago had been replaced by a plunge pool of icy water, a new reality. I was shocked throughout my being. There had to be a reasonable explanation for all of this, there just had to be. It was imperative I find out for certain, but how could I do so?

"Hi Mum!" My voice sounded normal as I spoke to her on the phone. How was that possible?

"Oh, hello, what's the weather like over there?" Mum invariably asked that question on the phone. Absently, I looked out of the window and was surprised to see it had started to rain heavily. April showers in May.

"Mum, I'm going to a prayer meeting this morning and I just wanted to ask if you need me to pray about anything?" *Oh God, that does sound lame?*

"No . . ." Mum's voice was often tentative and I was trying to read her tone, but she wasn't giving anything away. *Maybe I was wrong after all*, I thought, beginning to relax. *Of course you are!* spat my logical self. Mum didn't sound guarded or upset, but I decided to push a little harder just to be certain.

"Mum, are you sure there's nothing you want me to pray for?"

This time there was a delay in Mum's reply, and my last hope for a reprieve evaporated with her words. Despair settled on my heart like a thick blanket of snow, and our nightmare journey, which was to span almost two decades, had just begun.

"You could pray for your brother."

Somehow, I'd managed to drive home after the prayer meeting, collecting the children from school on the way, even though I was still almost paralysed with shock. Nancy Tromsness, who was hosting the meeting, had been alarmed when I'd arrived. She thought someone had died, I looked so crushed. She protected me from questions and from revelry, knowing I wouldn't be able to cope with either. She recognised that I wasn't yet ready to tell people what had happened. Of course, I would have to break this inconceivable news to my husband, Pat. He'd be home from work very soon and he'd be hungry. I told him to expect a nice dinner today because I wasn't going to classes – could I even manage to cook now? Would he still want his meal after I tell him this? Should I tell him before he eats, or afterwards? *Oh, God!*

Panic rose in my chest and I had an overpowering urge to run, to flee from this . . . but of course, I couldn't. I had responsibilities, the immediate one being the children, who had begun to do their homework in the kitchen. I could hear one of them calling for my help, and I knew I had to pull myself together, but my brain would not function. Would I have to break this news to them, too? Surely this will prove to be some crazy error and things will never reach that stage.

Poor Pat was still at work, innocently delivering kegs of beer for Beamish brewery. Idly, I wondered what area his route was today. Maybe Blarney? He'd be joking with the customers in that jovial way of his, grumbling about heavy traffic and the delivery company's management. He'd been a shop steward for some time, and often saw capitalist conspiracies as a consequence. Pat had always been anti-management and yet he'd married me, someone who had been in a management position in the catering supplies division of Musgrave's in Cork. He was always so proud to tell people I was in management – would he still be proud of his wife now? I didn't think so. I felt that I would have diminished in his eyes, become somehow tainted. Already, I was not what he'd hoped for. I was no longer employed, having chosen to go to college, which he tolerated. Pat couldn't see the purpose really, and he felt the responsibility of the financial pressure acutely.

It had been a mutual friend who'd introduced us. Marianne had been trying to get us together for ages, but I had resisted all her attempts to match-make. This guy lived at home with his parents, for goodness' sake! I didn't want to start a relationship with someone who hadn't even moved out of home yet, a mammy's boy. Then, on a night out in Ballincollig, in walked a tall, slim, rather handsome-looking man. He was dressed in blue jeans, a stripy shirt and a long grey cable-knit cardigan. His hands were shoved deep into the pockets of the jacket and he walked with a nonchalant air, like he was quite at home in this place.

Trying not to show my growing interest, I turned back to my friend, but our conversation was interrupted again when she, too, caught sight of him.

"Hey, Pat, come and sit over here," she called out, patting the seat beside her, a wicked grin on her face.

"Can I get both of you ladies a drink?"
And, as they say, the rest is history.

Marriage followed two years later and we bought a house in Ballincollig, just around the corner from Pat's family. Life seemed to be moving on a well-oiled track, going in the same direction as most other people's lives. One by one, the children arrived: Carine in 1985, Shane in 1987 and Emma Jane in 1990. Pat and I found ourselves working together day by day but growing further apart and, looking around me, I could see lots of other marriages going the same way. Life became humdrum, tedious and unfulfilling.

It was my psychiatrist who'd suggested college to me during my time in hospital in 1997.

"Why don't you enrol in a course at CIT? Maybe you could study psychology, I believe you'd do well at that," she informed me as she sat reading over my notes and scribbling additions to the page.

This was one of our one to one sessions, but I still looked around me to see who she was addressing, because she couldn't have meant me. I was a mental wreck, psychologically impaired. I'd signed myself into the psychiatric ward a few weeks ago when I felt like my mind was imploding.

The young doctor who'd interviewed me to assess my condition had asked, "Michelle, are you suicidal?"

Struggling up through the pain and fog, I thought for a moment before I answered, "No, but if I go home, I will die!"

The poor man had looked a bit nonplussed at that, but he took it seriously and admitted me to a ward. It was about six weeks later, after some R&R and one to ones with this impressive psychiatrist, that I found myself being assessed before going home.

Enrolling in college felt like a lifeline had been thrown to me. Someone highly educated and deemed worthy by dint of her expertise had viewed *me* and seen a real person, not the shadow I had become. I left hospital feeling confident and slightly rebellious;

I would stand up for myself from now on, I would protect my mental health and promote it in my children. I felt fragile, but whole.

Pat was very popular in Ballincollig. Jokes were his thing and everyone loved his humour. He could remember and retell gags so well, but he often made people laugh just because he was laughing so much himself he couldn't get to the ending – the punch-line would come out all wrong and in a fit of guffaws. Usually Pat would stop to indulge in some joke-telling one-upmanship with our next door neighbour, John, another joker, before coming indoors for his dinner. But there would be no laughing today. Something had happened that could crush the joy out of us forever.

Pat was someone who liked things to look right to the outside world. Perhaps that was why my depression seemed such an embarrassment to him. Somehow my illness belied his projection of our lives as 'The Happy Family'. His hostility towards my illness had been palpable; depression was never mentioned. In such an atmosphere, I didn't know how I could tell him that my brother might be involved in one of the highest profile crimes in recent British history. There is simply no precedent for events like this, no previous experience that can prepare you for being catapulted into the media glare. Where would it lead? I had no idea, but from that moment, it was my reality. My brother Barry had been arrested and I was still physically reeling after hearing his name on the news this morning. *Had it only been this morning?*

My head was fuzzy and not taking things in, even as my mind explored the possible ramifications to come. The feeling of panic was overwhelming. I wished that I might wake up and find this had never happened. *Oh please, Lord, let me wake up to another reality. I can't, I won't face this one. It's too much, don't ask it of me.*

The thought came again: *things like this don't happen to people like us.* We were just small, insignificant people; we would never rock the world with our achievements. We lived a little life: it was comfortable and predictable, even if it was boring at times. Pat and

I had a home that we'd worked hard to buy, a mortgage that we'd worked hard to pay off, and we had three children that we loved dearly. Why should there be an earthquake in our lives, a disaster threatening to annihilate all that we are? *Oh dear Lord, dear Lord, make this not be so.*

"Mum . . ." Emma Jane called out again, still asking for that help with her homework. "I'm not sure how to answer this."

"Let me see, darling. Oh, yes, if you . . ."

I dragged myself back to the here and now and tried to concentrate on the mundane. Was it possible to live like the world is still normal when there was a volcano waiting to blow in the middle of our lives? That day, I would seriously have welcomed my uneventful life back. I just longed to hold my head in my hands and wail!

Oh God, God, what am I to do?

2

Family Background

Our mother, Margaret Bourke, left home in County Limerick in 1951 at the tender age of fifteen to live with her uncle and aunt in London. This was not unusual in rural Ireland in the 1950s: jobs were scarce, with domestic servitude being the main option for girls from the country. The economic situation in Ireland and the demise of small rural farms led to a half a million young people leaving Ireland to seek work in that decade alone. In post-war England, migrant workers were needed and welcomed due to a severe labour shortage in Britain.

My grandfather was a corporal stationed in Dorset at Camp Bovington, a British army military base, when my father, Alfred Michael George, was born in 1930. The youngest of four children, the whole family lived and were educated on the camp in their early years, moving to London later. Young Alf was among the many children who were evacuated from London to the countryside during the Second World War. This was a traumatic time for children, separated from family and friends, often not even knowing where their siblings were or what was happening back home. Dad told me how the place he'd stayed in had been bombed, and that many of the children there hadn't survived. In 1947, Dad followed his father's footsteps and joined the army, where he served till he was discharged.

"Dad, can you tell me a bit about your time in the army? I really don't know anything. Were you conscripted?" I once asked him.

"No, I was not! I was an enlisted man," he said with both outrage and pride in his voice. He then went on to tell me about the Forgotten War, or Small War, where he'd served in Malaya until his discharge in 1954.

"It was a brutal conflict," he told me. "We British soldiers were sent out unprepared, and had to fight in extreme temperatures, in jungle conditions like those in Vietnam. Then in 1956, being an army reservist, I was recalled for the Suez Crisis where I served as a Royal Marine commando before Britain pulled out of the conflict."

Returning servicemen were not given any psychological help to deal with the effects of the trauma they had witnessed. They came home and tried to settle down to a normal life, but many were mentally scarred and their families suffered as a consequence.

In 1954, between his two terms of duty, Mum and Dad met and married. Mum was eighteen and Dad was twenty-four when they started married life together in two rooms in a house in Fulham. I was born on Good Friday, April 8th 1955, and Susan followed on February 5th 1958. It was recognised quite early on that Susan had epilepsy which was quite unstable, but the full effect of her intellectual disabilities were not actually confirmed until after we had moved from Fulham to White City in 1959. This move gave our little family more room to grow, and on Good Friday, 15th April 1960, Barry was born, just one week after my fifth birthday.

Susan and Barry were often put into my care, but looking after them became an increasingly difficult task as they became older and more likely to rebel against my authority.

One summer, when Barry was five, he and I went to the local outdoor swimming baths. In the summer holidays we could spend all day there for the princely sum of sixpence in old money. As usual, after I had been playing in the pool with friends, I'd bought us both lunch: a crispy bread roll with real butter and a thick hunk of cheddar cheese. We accompanied this with a large cup of beefy bouillon to warm us up. Barry had already eaten his lunch and had wandered off to play when I suddenly realised I couldn't see him or his distinctive Tarzan-patterned swimming trunks.

"Barry? Barry!" I called out, getting more and more frantic. I searched the dressing rooms and shouted into the men's toilet building, but to no avail. Then I spotted something floating, a child, face down on the top of the water. It was the unconscious body of my brother.

"Help, help!" I called to the lifeguard, who was sitting directly over the place where Barry was doing the dead man's float. He was chatting to a bevy of young women.

"Help me! I can't swim and my brother is drowning . . ."

He told me to stop mucking about and turned back to his adoring fan club. There wasn't time to do any thinking; I jumped into the deep part of the pool, spluttering and struggling to keep afloat, and reached out my arm to grab Barry by his trunks, pulling him to me. I thought we might both drown together now, because I really *couldn't* swim, and I hadn't the strength to lift either of us out of the pool. All at once there were hands everywhere, pulling us both to safety. A person sauntering by had seen Barry walking near the deep area as some kids ran past, knocking him into the pool. Barry was unconscious when we pulled him out, but came around shortly after and, at ten years old, I was left to dress him and walk him home after this ordeal. Mum didn't think about complaining to anyone, but after that I rarely got to spend a leisurely day by the pool. Barry was now terrified of water, and I was only allowed to take him to the kiddies' paddling pool in the park.

Friday the 12th August 1966 was a day I would never forget. I had charge of Susan and Barry for a typical outing to a local park. I had chosen to take us all to the adventure playground in East Acton, which was near Wormwood Scrubs Prison and Hammersmith Hospital. This was my favourite park.

After a few hours of scrambling around on the monkey bars, I gathered up my motley crew and we set out for the long walk home, spurred on by the lure of a hearty dinner which Mum would have ready and waiting for us. More important, of course, was getting Susan back for her medication. If she went too long between doses she could well start to fit, and if that happened while we were out I would be all alone to deal with it, whilst in charge of six-year-old Barry as well.

Braybrook Street ran along the edge of this common, colloquially referred to as 'The Scrubs'. The road curved almost in an 'L' shape from the prison walls to the playground. As we trekked home across the short grass along the boundary with the road, me herding my little flock and trying to keep us all together, we were surprised to hear what sounded like a car backfiring.

Rounding the bend, our ears were assaulted by the screaming of tyres squealing and spinning as a car sped past us, travelling in the direction we had come from. I grabbed Barry and Susan by the arm to stop them running towards the commotion and looked out into the road. There, amid the pandemonium of shouts and screams, I saw two men. One was lying on the tarmac and the other was hanging out of the driver's door of a stationary car, facing us. There was blood spattered on the road; both men were blood-stained and both were very obviously dead. At the time, I didn't realise there was a third body just out of my line of vision behind the car.

At just eleven years old, I felt ill-equipped to know what to do, but then who would know? This was not Chicago in the 1930s, this was West London in the 1960s, and this definitely wasn't an everyday experience.

I must get Susan and Barry away from here, I thought. *I don't know what will happen if they realise this is real. What shall I do?*

The hot August sun beat down as I started trying to guide my charges away from the terrible tableau before me. Susan wanted to investigate further, and I was scared the shock would bring on one of her seizures. How could I get this wilful eight-year-old to obey me? If she dug her heels in, I'd never shift her. Then inspiration struck . . .

"We can't go over there, Susan, they're making a film and we'll get in the way. They'll be angry with us if we muck up their movie."

Reluctantly, they both complied and trudged home with me. My legs were leaden from shock and I struggled with awful thoughts of what might have happened if we'd rounded that bend a couple of moments earlier.

"Mum! Mum! You won't believe what we saw today," I said, when the others were out of earshot. She didn't . . . not until the news came on the TV later that evening.

'News Flash: three policemen have been shot dead in West London.'

"Oh my goodness, you were telling the truth. Those poor men."

Most of my childhood had been taken up with looking after my siblings and I'd learnt to deal with Barry and Susan's challenging behaviour. These experiences meant I'd grown up very quickly. It was all simply the norm in our home. Of Course, the term Attention Deficit Hyperactivity Disorder, or ADHD, was not known when Barry was growing up, although a doctor had said he was hyperactive and had given Mum some pink syrup to help calm him so he, and we, could get some sleep. Other than that, there was no help for a family trying to cope with this disorder; there was no hope that things might get better, or advice on how to understand or deal with the difficult behaviours exhibited by such children. Children with ADHD were simply labelled as disruptive or disobedient. Often, like Barry, they were taken out of mainstream school and sent to schools for 'bad' kids.

Although Barry wasn't diagnosed with autism as a child, parents of children on the autistic spectrum will recognise the seemingly bizarre incidents we've had to deal with while Barry was growing up, such as when he was six and he leapt into a stationary milk float. These carts have a simple operation: step on the dead-man's switch and they move forward, step off and they stop. Barry could barely see out of the front windscreen, but he stepped onto this peddle and the vehicle lurched forward, heading for the extremely busy Westway motorway just twenty yards from us. Fear crossed his face when he realised he didn't know how to stop it. We all ran alongside, shouting, "Take your foot off, take your foot off . . ." Thankfully, he lifted his foot just before he reached the dangerous junction, and the cart stopped. The poor milkman looked like he might have a heart attack, and Barry was ashen, but it didn't put a stop to his adventures.

Another of his escapades landed him in hospital in an isolation ward. Barry had gone missing again; he often went off on his own. This time, he'd arrived home smelling of what seemed to be petrol. His white cotton shirt and grey short pants were soaked through, and when Dad removed them we could see that his abdomen was burnt and the skin was pink and raw and peeling off. He was unable to tell us what had happened to him, and he seemed dumbstruck with shock. All thoughts of telling him off were abandoned and he was rushed to Hammersmith Hospital immediately. I was allowed in to see him later. Just a little tot, lying in a bed with raised sides. His scorched tummy was uncovered because he could not have borne any weight on it. He lay white and lifeless in the glass room, alone and sad looking. I remember mentally saying my goodbyes to my six-year-old brother. I really thought that he was never coming home.

At the age of seven, he had been playing quietly in the bedroom that we three children shared when he emerged with a black face and hands, eyes like saucers, and ran out of the front door.

"You go in and see what he's done," Mum cried out to me. "I just can't." Mum stayed in the kitchen, wringing her hands, a fearful look in her eyes.

Cautiously opening the bedroom door, I stared in horror at the sight before me. The pretty floral print curtains were ablaze, smoke and flames billowed out of the open sash window. A matchbox and spent matches sat beside the timber window-frame which looked like charcoal, blackened and charred through. As I returned to the room with yet another bucket of water, I could hear the fire service approaching along Bloemfontein Road, sirens blaring. Someone else had seen the inferno pouring out from the back window and had reported it. By the time the fire brigade reached us, four floors up, I had put the flames out. The council then had to come and replace the window, since it could not be salvaged.

Mum and Dad separated acrimoniously in 1967, eventually divorcing in 1973. I was twelve at the time of separation, and we children stayed with Mum in the flats in White City. Then, two years later, all of the tenants were moved out of Creighton Close and relocated. The council wanted to renovate all the units, merging some to make larger apartments. The little community we'd been a part of for eight years was to be broken up, and we all mourned that loss. Nevertheless, we children could not believe our luck when we were resettled in an actual house . . . with an upstairs, a proper bathroom and everything! Running in through the front door of 79 Fitzneal Street, we were like small wild creatures let loose after being caged. Rushing around in all directions, our voices echoing in the empty rooms, we explored every nook and cranny, making discoveries: a pantry cupboard by the front door, a staircase that curved up leading to the bathroom, and we had a garden. *Wow!* We drew in our breath to inhale the fragrances of the new blue linoleum, old wood, and fresh paint. Mum just stood there in the hall looking at us, her expression one of bemusement.

Barry was given his own bedroom, upstairs at the back of the house, and Susan and I shared the large front bedroom next to his. Mum and her partner took the small room at the front of the property downstairs. When the house was first built in the 1930s, this was probably meant to be the dining room. There was also a sitting-room at the back of the building, and a tiny galley kitchen. We could not have been more excited. We thought we were rich!

Our little family were now embarking on a new journey, one that looked more positive, where we could start to write a new script for our lives. We had more space to move about in and there was a new local environment to explore in East Acton. I had more privacy now, too. I had a room to myself most of the time, because Susan was at boarding school in Hertfordshire.

With the confidence and inexperience of youth, I thought life would be so much better now that we'd moved, but if I thought our problems were now over, I was very wrong. Coming home from school one day, Mum met me at the door.

"Barry went out and I don't know where he is . . . he hasn't come back." Just as she told me this, the doorbell rang. Opening it, there stood the bold Barry, but he looked worried and held out a letter. It was from the manager of the local Woolworth's.

Dear Mrs George,

Please would you come to the store to speak with the Manager. Your son has been caught shoplifting, and we'd like to discuss this with you before we call the police.

Sincerely,
The Manager

Mum fell to pieces before our eyes.

"What have you done now, you idiot?" she shouted out to her son. "Can't you ever just behave yourself? I'm not going around there to talk to anyone, you can forget that!"

"But Mum, the man said he'd call the police if you don't go." Barry was now shaking with fear, his huge eyes brimming with unspilled tears.

"You'll have to go, Michelle, I can't do it. I can't face it." She was speaking to me! I was just fourteen years old, what could I do? Who would listen to me?

Dragging Barry by the arm, though I'd have preferred the neck, I marched him back to the Woolworth's store.

"What the hell were you thinking?" I bellowed at him, tugging at his arm some more. "How am I supposed to get you out of this? Why did you do it?"

Barry trudged along beside me and nervously began his explanation. "Mum is always crying and I wanted to make her feel better. I wanted to get her a present, but I didn't have any money," he told me with a worried expression. "I thought she'd be happy if I came home with chocolates and she wouldn't cry anymore or shout at me!"

We arrived at the shop, and at fourteen years old I had to try to justify what my nine-year-old brother had done. The manager was not inclined let us off lightly, though, and he was angry that our mother had not come herself. He described to me how Barry was stopped from leaving the store with his black bomber-style jacket bulging with chocolates: After Eights, a Dairy Box, and a couple of large bars of Cadbury's.

"He didn't even seem to realise that his plunder was clearly visible to anyone who looked!" the manager exclaimed in flabbergasted tones. "Why shouldn't I call the police, tell me that?"

Hanging my head in shame, I had to beg him to let Barry off for our mother's sake, giving Barry's account of how ill and how sad he thought she was. After some persuading the manager relented, but with the admonition that if Barry was ever caught again there would be no mercy shown. As we left the store, both of us in tears, I glanced back to see a look of sympathy and concern on the young manager's face as he watched us leave. To my knowledge, Barry never again took anything that didn't belong to him . . . he'd learned a valuable lesson.

Unfortunately, Barry did go on to acquire a criminal record. He was convicted of indecent assault in 1981 and was given a suspended sentence. In 1983, he was convicted of an attempted rape and was imprisoned for eighteen months, serving both sentences consecutively. I visited him in prison during this period, but it was not a comfortable time for Barry. I was incensed at his behaviour and let him know it.

Having moved to Ireland, it was rare for me to travel back to London. Fares were prohibitive, especially if you were travelling with children, so the next time I recall meeting up with Barry was in 1988 when I brought my two children to stay with Mum in London. With a lively three-and-a-half-year-old and a one-year-old, it was difficult to go anywhere, until Barry stepped in and carried my baby son Shane in a carrier on his back, which left my hands free to deal with my inquisitive little daughter Carine. We had such enjoyable times, going to parks and exhibitions and street carnivals. We attended an Asian Food Festival held on Shepherd's Bush Green, and the food from the vendors was hot and fragrant and really tasty.

Sadly, Barry and I lost touch after this, and I only ever spoke with him if he happened to be at Mum's when I phoned. I would always ask Mum, "How's Barry?" and Mum would respond, "He's fine." I didn't receive an invitation to his wedding when he married Itsuko Toide, a student from Japan, and I don't think Mum ever mentioned his divorce in 1990.

The next time I saw Barry was in 2000, when he was on remand for murder.

3

Charged: Remanded to Belmarsh Prison

After the shock of hearing about Barry's arrest, I made arrangements to go over to London. How expedient it would have been to just get up and go, but that couldn't be done. There was no possibility of getting away without telling people the reason, and I wasn't ready to do that yet. Since no one knew Barry Bulsara was related to me, I was still hoping that it would all blow over and that no one need know we were implicated in this mayhem. Money was also an issue, and we had to rob Peter to pay Paul to get the money together for a flight.

Barry had appointed his own solicitor, Ms Marilyn Etienne, in place of the duty solicitor offered to him by the police. He had sought Marilyn's help before, with a claim against a driver who had knocked him off his bicycle and injured him. Even though she had not won him any compensation, he still had faith in her to help him with this charge. I had yet to meet her and had no opinion, but she did phone me regularly to update me on Barry's situation. During one of these phone calls, she had reassured me that the police would have to release Barry as they had no evidence to hold him. This was joy to my ears! I wouldn't have to go England now; the case would collapse and never come before a judge. Our nightmare was to be short lived after all. I was elated, and planned a little retail therapy for the following day.

Hello Moto . . . my mobile phone sang out in my bag. I was walking around Marks and Spencer's in Cork City and quickly answered the call from Marilyn, hoping she had news of Barry's imminent release.

"Michelle . . . I don't know how to tell you this, but they are charging Barry with murder."

I had been looking at the gaily-coloured fashions for the season and had been quite engrossed in my reverie, but suddenly all I could see were shadows and the colour grey. My vision became tunnelled and my surroundings seemed to shrink, as though I had been lifted out of this spacious store and was now enclosed in a tiny room. The urge to pace was unbearable.

"What? How?"

I began to move now, pacing slowly up and down the aisles of the fashion department, my mobile phone clamped tightly to my right ear and my other hand cupping the left side of my head to block out the ambient sounds around me. Normal sounds of people doing normal things. Women chattering about holidays to come and outfits to buy, children playing near the escalator, chirruping with joy as they rode up and struggled back down against the flow.

"Marilyn, how did this happen?"

By now the terror had started to rise in my chest and I thought it would burst. Surely everyone around me could see my panic, would know that I felt like a trapped animal. But no one looked my way, even when I blindly walked across their paths. They were oblivious to my fear and anxiety.

Marilyn was speaking again and I tried to find a spot where the signal was clearer.

". . . on his coat."

"Say that again, Marilyn, I didn't catch it."

"Sorry, Michelle, I said they've found a single particle of firearms discharge residue on his coat. They say it matches the residue on Jill's hair."

Dear Lord, did he do it? My mind was racing as I launched my desperate thoughts to God.

"Marilyn, what does this mean?" Now I was truly afraid.

"No, well, it's ridiculous really," Marilyn asserted. "It doesn't mean anything, and it's all wrong anyway: forensics didn't examine the coat until after the police had opened the sealed evidence bag and had taken the coat to a police photographic laboratory."

"What? They can't do that!" My mind was desperately trying to find some sense in all of this. "Everyone and his dog knows you can't open evidence bags, Marilyn, even a child knows that! Surely it will have to be thrown out?" Somehow I found myself outside of the store, on St. Patrick's Street, pacing to keep from completely breaking down.

"The finding has no integrity as evidence, Michelle, but it gave the police the reason they needed to be able to charge him. Before they found this, they were going to have to let him go." Marilyn tried to assure me that all would still go well, but it sounded to me as if we were dealing with a police force that was either stupid or desperate.

"Are you still coming to London, Michelle?" Marilyn asked.

"Yes, I suppose I'll have to, Marilyn, though we can ill afford it. Anyway, I'll phone you when I arrive."

Ringing off, I stumbled back to the car park, located my car through the mist of panic that surrounded me, and drove back to Ballincollig half-drunk with shock. Looking back, I can see that Marilyn was both right and wrong. Wrong because Barry *was* convicted due to the way the prosecutor in the trial presented this one microscopic particle to the jury. Right, because this speck, which became the most famous speck in recent legal history, would lead to Barry's conviction being quashed in 2007 because it was evidentially neutral.

Barry was charged and remanded to Belmarsh Prison to await trial. Naïvely, I was under the mistaken belief that someone innocent until proven guilty would be housed in a less repressive part of the prison, with a freer system for visitors, and could expect different treatment from that of convicted persons. Oh boy, was I in for a rude awakening! Barry had been remanded as a provisional Cat

A prisoner, a category reserved for dangerous criminals or those who were at high risk of escaping. This seemed fair enough, since the charge was murder, but we fully expected this to be reviewed and that he would then be classified as a Cat B or Cat C Prisoner, since he was not dangerous and posed no flight risk. It was not reviewed, and he remained a Cat A prisoner, someone regularly locked up for 23 out of 24 hours a day. In Britain, we look at other countries that lock people up in this way and we say they are barbaric, and that this infringes people's human rights . . . but this goes on in our prisons all the time.

Anyway, escape would have been unthinkable for Barry, since he couldn't go anywhere without causing some sort of disruption. His planning and sequencing abilities are highly impaired, and his physical coordination is clumsy and graceless, so escape from a high security prison was an impossibility. However, in Barry's case, the British justice system's propaganda machine was engaged and working at full throttle. It suited the police and the system to have it known to the public that Barry George was a Cat A prisoner, because this showed that he was considered highly dangerous, therefore reinforcing the idea that he was a guilty man. In the eyes of the public, he became the murderer, a heinous fiend who had been apprehended after he had cleverly evaded the police for a whole year, whilst still living in the same area – the same apartment, even! The police had captured their criminal mastermind.

Mum was Barry's first visitor to Belmarsh Prison, and as such, the rules surrounding visits were clarified to her. It was explained that as Barry's close family, she would be required to attend one 'closed' visit, then after that her visits would be 'open'. After an initial closed one, I too would have open visits. However, Barry's uncle, Mike, was considered extended family and was not a UK resident, so he would have to wait until his clearance papers came through before being allowed open visits.

Closed visits are reserved for people who are not family members, people still awaiting clearance, and for those who have been caught with drugs or contraband in the past and consequently cannot be allowed physical access. It is also for dangerous or violent prisoners. For these visits, the visitor is conducted to a tiny room, about six by eight feet. There, behind the waist-high wall topped with a thick and murky Perspex window, is another room that mirrors this one. This is where the prisoner sits, separated from his visitors. There are no holes in this foggy grey windowpane for sound to travel through. To hear clearly, one must pick up the dirty-looking phone from the wall and put it up to their head. In attendance with the prisoner is a guard who overhears all conversations.

During my first visit, it was easy to see that Barry was delighted at my being there, but equally he was distressed at having to have a closed visit. He would not pick up the handset, but then, neither would I. He because of his concern about lack of privacy, I because of my aversion to its filthy state. Therefore, we had to shout and gesticulate to each other to communicate. Mum sat quietly by my side looking less than alive, she was so frail. Despite all of this, I managed to convey to Barry that we would fight, and not give up fighting till he was freed.

This was an unlikely setting for two siblings to discover that they had both taken a similar journey in their otherwise disparate lives. We had both decided to follow Jesus, to be committed Christians, and we both now attended Baptist churches. Barry was physically bouncing to tell me this news. It was the second most important thing he wanted to tell me, with the first being that this was all a mistake, that he hadn't killed Jill Dando. I had been going to ask him that, but he pre-empted me. It rather took the edge off his revelation when I told him that I had also become a Baptist some years earlier, and had been baptised a couple of years later. Barry's Believer's Baptism was planned to coincide with the return of his friend, a deacon in his church named Dolores Smith, who was due back from Jamaica after her holiday. He was arrested and charged before he could be baptised.

Barry, looking lost and sad and worried, placed his hand flat against the nearly opaque glass, fingers splayed, as if to touch us on the other side. My heart felt wrenched from my chest and I followed his lead, pressing my hand to the glass, too, and willing it to melt away under our touch.

"Don't worry, Barry. We know you didn't do it, and you can't be found guilty if there is no evidence against you."

How naive can one person be?

Just one closed visit. That's what I had been told. As Barry's close family, there was no need for prior clearance, though I did fill in all the paperwork and hand delivered it to the Gardaí in my home village.

"Don't worry, Mrs Diskin. I will personally complete this and post it back ASAP," the detective assured me.

Months later, I was still on closed visits. Of all people, it was actually a journalist from the Daily Mirror who would help me with this. Whilst on a visit to my home to procure an interview for his paper, I was lamenting the fact that I was still on these closed visits. Various friends and family, such as Mike, could visit Barry in the main visitors' hall. My closed visits distressed Barry because whenever I would attend, all of us would have to go to the dirty glass room again. If I wasn't there, they could have had an open visit. This made me feel guilty, but having travelled over from Ireland, I couldn't miss an opportunity to see him.

This compassionate journalist was so moved that, rooting around in his briefcase, he located an unlisted telephone number for Hammersmith Police Station, a line used by journalists.

"Ring this number, Michelle, but don't say where you got it from. It should get you through to someone who can check on your status."

He had come for a story and had started by using all his wiles to get one, but he'd ended up trying to help us instead. I had previously asked at the prison why were my visits still closed, and I was told by security personnel that it was the police who decided who was allowed open visits. However, when I'd asked the police,

I was told it was up to the prison service and had nothing to do with them. Around and around it went, with no answer, till I felt dizzy and almost ready to give up.

Almost.

A couple of days after being given the unlisted number, I dialled it with some trepidation. Who would answer, and how would they treat me? Should I be subservient and meek, or should I go on the offensive, demanding my right to information? Nothing in my life had prepared me for this type of combat.

"Hammersmith Police Station, PC Smith speaking, how can I help you?" The voice sounded very young and friendly.

"May I speak with someone who can explain why I have not been cleared for prison visits, please?" I enquired. "I've been on closed visits to my brother for months, even though I was told that I wouldn't have to wait. I don't have a criminal record, so I can't understand the delay."

I gave as much information as I could to this nice young woman in the hope that she could help me without calling a senior officer. I was very concerned that I'd be told off for using this unlisted number and that the call would be ended. Also, my innate respect and deference to the authority of the police made it feel wrong to be interrogating them.

Tap, tap, tap, shuffle, click, went the sound of a keyboard and mouse as the young PC asked questions and entered my answers on her computer.

"It would seem that you *are* cleared, Mrs Diskin. You've been cleared since the beginning," she responded, her manner cheerful and open, her voice sounding somewhat puzzled.

It worked, I thought with relief, *I've accessed the information I needed*. Then my brain started whirring as I realised the implication. I should not have been kept on closed visits all these months, so who had authorised this?

"Thank you so much for your help, PC Smith, it's much appreciated. I wonder, though, can you see why I've been kept on closed visits? The prison said it was the police who required it." I had nothing to lose by asking, but I was dreading the possible battle to come.

PC Smith started interrogating her computer again. Then I heard an officer call her away from the phone, and I was put on hold. *Oh no, what now,* I thought. *Is this where I get into trouble?*

"Hello, Mrs Diskin? PC Smith again, I'm sorry for that delay. It seems I was mistaken; you're not cleared yet. Your papers have not been returned by the Irish Police." The hesitancy in her voice made me think she'd just been reprimanded for letting the cat out of the bag, and told to retract what she'd said. *What are they trying to pull now?*

"I'm sorry, PC Smith, but it isn't necessary for me as a close family member to have police clearance. Other people who are just friends from his church have been able to visit openly for months. I am the only person on this strict regime! Please can you tell me who I need to speak with to sort this out? May I speak with your superior, please?"

My heart was racing with both apprehension and with sheer white anger. I knew I was being given the run-around again, that this officer had been told to change her story. Well, I wasn't giving up now.

Putting me on hold again, the young officer went off to see what else could be done.

"Sorry again, Mrs Diskin, but I've been told it's up to the prison service to decide who has open visits and who doesn't. You'll have to take it up with them. I'm afraid I can't help you any further, goodbye." She ended the call before I could reply.

I was left churning with rage. Our family believe this was a conspiracy to keep me away from Barry and a ploy to undermine his confidence. My presence seemed to buoy him up, to bring him hope and keep his strength going for the fight ahead. Somehow, I had been deemed a danger to a legal process that was determined to ensnare him. Unimportant me . . . a danger.

Getting into Belmarsh Prison for a visit is an ordeal in itself and Mum found it particularly onerous, but she would have stripped naked and walked over hot coals to see her boy.

"Did Mike write out the route for you, Mum?" I knew he'd done this for her because he'd told me, but she still seemed confused and worried about the journey.

"I wish there was a bus I could take, I always hated the underground . . . I can't find my way around, I'm scared I'll get lost or something."

Poor Mum. In all the years that I can remember, she had only been on the underground a handful of times, and even then she'd had someone else as navigator. Now she was having to take the underground with two changes, plus use the Docklands Light Rail and then a bus. In total, the journey took two hours, just to get across London to Belmarsh. With two hours to get there, one hour waiting to get into the prison, a two hour visit – if it wasn't cut short by the prison – and two hours back, that was seven hours just for one visit. A whole day's work!

"I'll be over in a few days, Mum, then we can go together," I assured her. "I think there is a less confusing route that cuts out one of the changes for you, we'll check that out." It was a worry to hear the fear in Mum's voice; she had started to sound so frail.

"You can check out if there's a cheaper way, too," she blurted out. "It's *so expensive!* They gave me a form to fill in to get help with fares, but I don't qualify because I worked all those years ago and I get a small pension from my job. If I'd never worked, they would pay most of my fare for me. It makes me so mad! All them people who never worked a day in their lives and they claim everything under the sun. My son didn't do this thing but I have to pay out everything myself, with no help!"

Mum was right; I'd checked it all out for her. She used to work as a home-help in the Hammersmith and Fulham borough, which meant she didn't qualify for assistance. Even though Barry was innocent, she, and all of us, would have to stump up a huge financial outlay just to support him. I did a rough calculation in

2007, factoring in Mum's fares to visit Barry, the money she sent to him for what's called The Tuck Shop, the only place inmates can purchase shaving gear, deodorant and the 'tuck' they often use instead of the bland meals. Then the money Mike sent to Barry and the cost of sending in clothing and shoes, my UK train tickets and airfares, my expenses for being away from home, plus phone calls to and from Ireland. All of this, over the course of the eight years leading up to Barry's release, added up to over fifty thousand pounds. This is money that will never be reimbursed to us. Families of the wrongfully convicted do not receive compensation.

"Mum, has the visiting order arrived yet?" The VO was an essential part of the paperwork needed for visits to take place.

"Yes, it arrived yesterday. Shall I phone to book a visit for the Friday or Saturday?" Thank goodness Mum would do this. If I'd had to do this from Ireland it would have cost a packet, because you're left on hold for ages! Having received a VO from a prisoner is not enough to be able to visit. A visitor must pre-book a date and time via the bookings phone line, which could mean ringing and ringing because this line is always so busy. No leeway would be given if this step was not carried out.

Mum knew the drill. Sometimes a friend or relative accompanied Mum to the prison and they'd wait in the Visitors' Centre, then travel back with her. On these visits Mum seemed to be less stressed out, and therefore less depressed at the bleakness of it all.

"Don't forget you need four passport photos and your birth certificate. Bring your passport, too, and two utility bills, and they must be from the last three months or they won't accept them. I think you should bring your driving license as well, because they can be very picky about photos." Mum reeled off the list of paperwork items I would need just to enter the facility.

Coming from Ireland, I had to produce extra 'proof of address' documentation. Mum didn't have to bring this much paperwork with her for every visit, thank goodness.

"Okay, Mum, see you next week. Give my love to everybody, and especially to the old ladies," I said, ringing off with a reference to the elderly women that Mum would visit on a regular basis. Like all of us, she never viewed herself in this category, even though some of her old ladies were younger than herself.

The security procedures employed at the Visitors' Centre (located just outside of the prison building's walls) make for a fraught experience for all visitors. Solicitors, individuals and families must select a locker to store bags and personal effects in when they arrive. There is a little play area here in the Belmarsh Centre for small children, toilet facilities with baby-changing areas, and a pleasant café where one can buy snacks and beverages at non-profit prices and sit in fairly convivial surroundings. Having checked in with security, one has to wait the best part of an hour before the main checks are done, so it's important that this area is available for visitors.

The Visitors' Centre is run by the children's charity, Spurgeons, and staffed by volunteers, aka 'Angels'. They do a wonderful job of supporting all the people who come through the centre, especially those with children who find themselves having to pass through this high security environment. These Angels lend a helping hand and a shoulder to cry on, as I know from my own experience. There is no praise high enough for these kind-hearted people.

Part of the check in procedure is the hand-stamp. An officer, having checked all of your documentation, will then rubber-stamp the back of your hand. They use a yellow substance that has a distinctive and strong odour, rather like the carbolic soap we used in the 50s, or a disinfectant, and it always itched like crazy on my skin. They use a similar system in night clubs and at concerts to check who's going in and out. The mark of the stamp glows under special UV lamps and it will be checked going in and coming out of the prison. The first thing I always wanted to do upon leaving the prison was to rush to the toilets and scrub off this scratchy symbol of shame with plenty of soap and water.

It's essential to bring everything exactly as advised on the VO to the check in; if anything is missing or incorrect, even if the error is on the prison's side, your visit will be refused.

On one of my lone visits, I witnessed an elderly man rush in to the centre, breathless from his journey. A taxi had dropped him off at the door and the driver had helped him in with his luggage because he had difficulty walking and carrying his suitcases. He had arrived directly from the airport. This stately-looking Asian man was reduced to crying, sobbing unashamedly in the Visitors' Centre, because his visit was refused. He thought it was because he was late, but it wasn't. He had travelled from India that day to see his son who was remanded to Belmarsh Prison. I overheard the conversation between him and the officers.

"I am sorry to be late, sir, but I have come from India today. I have this paper, and I have my passport, they are here. I want to see my son, please."

His voice was thickly accented, as though he was not used to conversing in English. This country was alien to him, let alone this prison environment, and he wore a worried countenance.

Alas, he had come ill-prepared: he didn't have the utility bills with him for proof of address. There was no compassion shown to him. The pain and confusion etched into his face meant nothing to 'the system' and he was told to go. It should have been possible, at security's discretion, for him to have a closed visit, since he *was* on the visitor's list and was expected. His son would be awaiting his arrival, but this solution was not offered. He could not have his visit, and so his son would wait in vain. His son would not even know why his dad hadn't come, would not know if his dad had even arrived in the country, or was still in India . . . he would be told nothing. When I left the centre to go for my visit, this hapless, broken father was being comforted by a volunteer Angel in the now empty Visitors' Centre.

The next stage in this unyielding visits process was the walk over to the prison building, this time for physical security checks. Again, the paperwork that had just been screened had to be rechecked and the hand-stamp illuminated and viewed. If you were found wanting in any way, it resulted in you having to walk back to the Visitors' Centre to have it put right, or even a refusal to visit. "You can't come in with that!" Mum was told once. "You have to go back to the Visitors' Centre and leave it there." The infringement? The brooch on her lapel. I was also sent back once with a bangle which I had forgotten to take off. No one is exempt, no one is spared. Young mothers could not take in a baby-bag with necessities, just a bottle and a nappy. It seems someone had once tried to smuggle drugs in this way, so security was tightened for everyone. All of this security is completely understandable, but nevertheless painful, and it is all the more distressing when the person being visited has not committed a crime: the injustice of the invasive system is heightened.

Having successfully navigated the first of the hurdles, it's now time to straddle even higher jumps. This was where the real humiliation was felt. Airport security has taken some of the sting out of this now, since we all understand the need for protection from terrorist attacks and are used to security checks, but it is still a painful and undignified process. Shoes, jackets and belts must come off and be put through the x-ray machine, along with the plastic bag of coins you're allowed to take in to buy coffees and snacks. The only jewellery allowed is a watch and a wedding ring. Garments are also hand-searched: seams, pockets, hems, collars. If any contraband is found then it's back through the system you've just navigated to have said infringement put right.

Onwards and upwards: you've successfully manoeuvred your way through the x-ray system. So far, so good. Now for the invasion of your person. The next part of the process is similar to airport security, but much more invasive and humiliating. Having passed through the airport-style security scanner, it was time to move on to the next ordeal. Arms outstretched, an officer of your gender gives you a frisk, wearing latex gloves for hygiene purposes. Everything has to be checked in this examination, from the top of your head, through your hair, in and behind the ears, under the arms and along each sleeve, palms up, palms down. Then around the breasts, checking the bra area, feeling around any under-wires and back hooks. Next, the waistband of your jeans or skirt is interrogated with probing fingers, then hands slide down each leg, inside and out, all the way to the ankles.

"Open your mouth and lift your tongue, please . . . wiggle it, to the left, to the right," the officer commands as she peers into this cavern, seeking contraband.

Next, you have to prove that your watch is operational. It is advisable to have a second hand on it, or you'll have to wait a minute or so until some movement is spotted. *OK*, you think to yourself. *Surely now it's all finished.*

"Lift up your foot and show me the soles of your feet," is the next order. I've seen my elderly mother almost topple over as she tried to comply with this one, and I learned not to wear tights that might develop a hole in the toe . . . so embarrassing.

At last. Now it's okay to collect our trays of x-rayed belongings and go over to the bench to get dressed again. *Why does it always seem to take longer to button up and to tie my shoes when I'm here than it does at home?* I wonder as I fumble about in my haste. Stealing a look at mum I could see that she's struggling too, and wearing that bemused and lost look again. She sighs a lot these days.

Hail, rain or snow, we all walk to the next building, often still struggling with shoes or belts as we try to finish dressing. Hail, rain or snow, we all wait for the officer inside to open the next security pod so we can get in from the elements. Once inside, we'll again show our paperwork and hand-stamps. If anything is wrong . . . you know the way back!

From there, it is possible to see the visiting room, a huge hall with modular tables and chairs bolted to the floor. It was just through those doors to the left . . . but wait, not yet. We are directed to take a seat on the cold and slippery moulded plastic seating, welded to the floor in rows and colour-blocks. Eventually, our names are called out and we can line up to enter. *Am I there yet?* Weariness floods in, caused not just by the passage of time, but by the mind-numbing processes that have to be endured. Frequently, I would sit there, idly watching the sniffer dogs as they checked out the line of people waiting to go in. They wove in and out around the feet of adults and children alike. Some children became very nervous around the dogs and clung tightly to their parent's legs, but others took it all in their stride.

Oh! I pondered as I watched them, mesmerised. *Why has that dog sat down and not moved again? Uh oh, someone has been sent back.* The dogs were there to detect the odour of drugs and that one had obviously smelled something. The detected person was offered a closed visit due to the dog's response, but declined it and left the prison without a visit. This once happened to Mike when we were all waiting to see Barry. Mike hates drugs, but the dog detected something so he, and we, were offered a closed visit. Feeling rightly miffed, Mike declined so that Mum and I could have a proper visit with Barry. Apparently all that was needed for the dog to find an odour was for Mike to have sat somewhere a user had sat.

"He could easily have picked up microscopic particles on his clothes from the pub," I explained to Mum, who had been upset for Mike.

People on open visits are permitted one hug with the inmate on arrival, then one again on departure. That's all the touching allowed, but Barry was sometimes uncomfortable even with this. "They don't like it," he'd say, indicating the officers patrolling the room.

"Barry," I would say in my loudest normal voice, "we are not doing anything that's not allowed, so *no one* is going to rob you of this right!" He would also ask me to speak quietly. It seems the guards had referred to me in derogatory terms because of my Irish accent after visits were over. It did make me so mad to see how intimidated Barry felt by the system.

The patrolling guards watched and listened in as and when they pleased, making it difficult to discuss legal strategies or how we were going to fight this trumped-up charge . . . but it had to be done here, as there was nowhere else for us to talk. If the prisoner stood up, the guards would shout, "Sit down!" If we sat in the wrong colour-coded seat they would call out, "Other chairs!"

In the open visits hall we could buy tea, coffee, fizzy drinks and packaged snacks from The Tuck Shop, and the Angels who ran this facility were very kind and non-judgmental. It was usual to see a gaggle of children surrounding the counter buying treats while mums and dads took the chance to talk.

These visiting times were arduous, but the alternative, not seeing Barry, was far worse. Although there were tough times and hard conversations to be had in those visits, they were worth it if they helped him to fight on. We would endure whatever we had to to support him.

4

Broken

He's Irish!

A Sunday newspaper had found out Barry's birth surname, George, and that's when the media circus started with a vengeance. They tracked Mum down to her home, and it seemed that every print publication and TV channel in the UK was represented in the encampment outside the house, where they stayed for thirteen days straight. She became a prisoner in her own home. If she twitched a curtain, cameras flashed at the windows. If she had to answer the front door, people ran at her with microphones and TV cameras trying to get 'the scoop' interview with the 'killer's mother'. Mum found herself living in a nightmare realm of media intimidation.

Before this, Mum would have thrown open her bedroom curtains and opened the windows to let the day in as soon as she arose. Now they both had to remain firmly closed. The people outside, waiting for their exposé, spent their time chattering loudly, enjoying packed meals and takeaway coffees and laughing and joking to pass the time. As soon as anyone noticed signs of life within the house, they would shout out to each other.

"Look, look! Up at the window . . . there she is!"

It was as though she were a convicted killer on the run, and they had discovered her hiding place. The doorbell kept ringing, the knocker was pounded, they tapped loudly on the front room window, shouting.

"Mrs George, why won't you speak to us?"

"Tell us, Mrs George, is he guilty?"

She was mercilessly tricked by one journalist seeking a story.

"Mrs George, I'm investigating the murder of Jill Dando, may I speak with you?"

Mum, thinking he was a Met Police detective, opened the door to find a news reporter thrusting a microphone in her face and spewing questions, while a cameraman was already filming her. Another photographer saw a photo opportunity and snapped her picture. The photo was printed on the front page of the Daily Mail the next day. It was a photo of a shocked, terrified and vulnerable elderly woman, clutching her dressing gown about her throat with her hair awry. It was cruel and unjustifiable. What had this intensely private woman done to deserve this?

This was repulsive behaviour. When I'd booked my trip to London, there didn't seem to be a burning need to get there: all was quiet, we were still unknowns. My plane ticket couldn't be changed now, so I couldn't get to Mum for another three weeks. All any of us could do was phone her as often as possible to see that she was okay. I felt angry and powerless when she said she could not leave her house for any purpose. For a deeply reserved person this intrusion was unbearable, and if her neighbours hadn't rallied round and passed milk, bread and cat food over the back fence, she and her beloved cat Sheba could have starved to death in there while the media circus played on outside her door.

Thankfully, Mum got through this horrendous period, thanks in no small part to all the family and friends who phoned and wrote letters to her.

On my first visit to Mum, the police rang her and I answered.

"Mum can't speak right now, maybe I can help?"

The officer went on to introduce himself then asked if I would be willing to provide a character reference to help my brother. This sounded interesting: here was an officer who seemed to think there may be doubt about Barry's guilt.

"Yes, I'll gladly do anything I can to help my brother, who is, of course, innocent of this crime, but not until after I've spoken with his solicitor."

On phoning Marilyn I was quickly disabused of the thought that this would help Barry. "Michelle, the only people who will be helped by anything you say to the police will be the prosecution, and you could find yourself being called as a prosecution witness against your brother."

Oh my goodness, what a bombshell! I could so easily have offered to do this. In fact, one of our aunts did just that, and a few weeks later a PC called to her home to ask to sign her statement.

"I didn't make a statement, it was a character reference!" she replied sharply. She wasn't going to have the wool pulled over her eyes.

"They are the same thing, and you may be called in to court to give evidence for the prosecution," the young PC informed her.

She phoned me in anger and alarm. "How dare they! He's innocent, and I just wanted them to understand his difficulties." She had always trusted the police, but now she was disillusioned and tremulous. Mercifully, she was never called into court.

Arriving back in Cork after a visit to see Mum and Barry, I felt enormously relieved to be home. I really loved our village, and it was great to be in my own home with my gorgeous children. I could sleep in my own bed, with my own things around me, and of course, the children really needed their mum. I really needed them, too. I always felt so guilty when I had to go back to England to work for Barry, and so planning pleasurable things to do as a family, such as a picnic or a trip to a country park, was especially enjoyable. This was what I was doing when the phone rang, and the caller ID showed it was a withheld number from the UK. Another journalist?

It wasn't. It was my mother's best friend, Maura.

"Hi Maura, how are you? Is everything OK?" I asked, feeling a bit puzzled. Why would Maura be ringing me now? It was only a few days since I had last seen her.

"Michelle, I couldn't get your mother on the phone today, so I called around . . . I had to use my key to get in."

My blood froze, and my head started to spin. What had she found? I was almost too scared to speculate, even as my brain went racing ahead to ready me for the worst news. Standing rooted to the spot, I awaited the emotional blow that would knock me sideways. "Your mother is ill."

Relief flooded through me and I sought a place to sit down quickly. *She's alive! Oh, thank you, God.*

"How ill is she, Maura? Do I need to come over?" I asked, with more calm than I felt. *Oh please God, no,* I prayed. *I was with Mum just a few days ago, I've only just come back and started to settle in with my family . . . surely her doctor can sort this out without my being there?*

"That has to be your decision, Michelle, but I found her and the poor cat in a bad way. She must have become ill very quickly . . . she hasn't fed herself or drunk anything, nor fed the cat or let it out. I've called the doctor, but they're not keen to listen to me. They don't class me as important enough. I tell you this, that woman cannot be left in this state. I've gone around and cleaned up as much of the mess as I can, but I can't take responsibility for her in this condition." I could hear the anger, fear and frustration in Maura's voice.

Oh dear God, here we go again. When will I get some breathing space? Now I will have to tell Pat and the children that I'm leaving, and so soon. How much more of this can my kids take? How much more will my husband stand for?

My insides were churning, and all the blood seemed to have drained out of me, leaving me shivering. I started my now habitual response to stress, pacing up and down the tiled kitchen floor. I felt as though I was being rent in two! If only there could have been two of me: one at home in Ireland, enjoying the life and responsibilities of a wife and a mother, the other one in the UK, fighting for Barry and supporting Mum. *God help me,* I implored. Yet again I felt utterly overwhelmed, but of course, I had to go.

Maura would say no more, but then, knowing that our phones were being tapped, she was right. We had nothing to hide where the case was concerned, but Mum certainly had a right to privacy and we had to protect her. I offered up one last prayer, then logged on to the Aer Lingus website and booked my flight, knowing that we had just one week's wages left in our bank account.

"Hi Mum, I'm here . . ." I called out in a cheery voice as I let myself into the house. There was no answer from Mum, but Maura came out from the sitting room.

"Your mother is upstairs in bed," she told me. "I've given her a cup of tea, but I couldn't get her to eat anything. She's like a little bird, and she's completely confused, keeps talking about Susan as if she's still alive." My sister, Susan, had died in 1987 in an epileptic seizure. "The poor cat is in a terrible state, too, look at her."

Sheba was sitting near the back window, but I would have been hard pressed to recognise her in this poor wretched thing before me. We always teased Mum that her cat should be known as 'fat-cat', because before Mum had even had her first cup of tea in the morning, that cat would have been almost force-fed an array of foods. Sheba was a big fat tabby queen, but this poor creature was skin and bone, and in just a few days. *How had this happened?* There had been no indication before I left; nothing to warn me that Mum wasn't coping.

"I don't know what would have happened to that woman if I hadn't had a key to get in here. Thank God she didn't shoot the bolt on the front door, or she could have been dead in that chair," Maura said, pointing to the dark blue leather couch. "And that lot . . ." She wrinkled up her face with a look of distain, and waved her arm to indicate the recent encampment of journalists. "They wouldn't have given a tinker's-damn. Just more b***** tripe for them papers!"

We walked into the front bedroom to see Mum, Maura pointing out to me where she had had to clean up along the way. Obviously, unable to get out, the cat had messed. Mum had tried feebly to clear it up, but had only managed to smear the mess everywhere and trail it throughout the house. This was scary. How could I not have seen any signs of this happening?

"Margaret, are you awake?" Maura tried to rouse Mum. "Michelle is here, your daughter."

The woman in the bed seemed to pull herself out of a deep torpor. Her expression was blank, until a childlike smile spread across her face. A trusting look, but with a tremor of uncertainty.

"Hello . . ." Mum spoke to me in a drawn out, sing-song voice, much like the one she may have used when she was a wide-eyed little girl back in Limerick. It was totally at odds with the shrewd, canny woman I had known all my life.

Trying to get more than a hushed word from Mum proved impossible, and it was an eerie feeling talking over her as she looked from one of us to the other uncomprehendingly. The doctor would have to come. This was something I could not deal with on my own; I was totally out of my depth here.

The child in the bed gripped the sheets with tremulous hands and smiled shyly.

"Mrs Diskin, your mother is a very sick woman. She has dementia and will have to go into hospital. However, we have a problem," the doctor explained. "If she doesn't agree to go in herself, she will have to be sectioned, and I'll have to call another doctor to sign the papers. The ambulance is on its way now." The doctor from Mum's GP surgery was not one I recalled meeting before, but he had a kindly face under today's furrowed brow.

"Mrs George, do you know who I am?" the doctor asked Mum. She smiled a pretty little smile, with just a hint of pleading in her eyes. The doctor tried again. "You are very sick, Mrs George, and you need to be where we can help you. Do you understand?" A nod, and then a drifting off to . . . wherever again.

"Mrs George," he gently roused her again. "Will you go to the hospital for us?"

I waited with bated breath. *Oh please, Mum, don't make them section you. Agree, please agree,* I silently implored her, and then I raised a prayer of pleading to Jesus.

Another nod from Mum, accompanied by an almost imperceptibly whispered "Yes" saved her from the ignominy of losing her liberty and effectively becoming as much a prisoner as her son. She would not now have to be sectioned under the Mental Health Act, and we all breathed a sigh of relief. I hurriedly packed a bag for Mum as we waited for the ambulance to arrive.

"Margaret, you're as light as a feather," quipped one of the jovial ambulance crew. "We'd better make sure you don't blow away."

Carefully strapping their compliant patient into the upright ambulance chair and wrapping her in some blankets, they gently lifted her into the back of the vehicle and secured the seat in place. She was oblivious to the interested looks from concerned neighbours who lined the pavement or looked out from upstairs windows. I was so glad that she would not have to bear their pitying looks, nor feel the mortification at being 'carted off to the funny farm', as she would have called it. The neighbours, for their part, were truly sorry to see Mum so ill.

The child being lifted into the ambulance looked back to where her firstborn was standing, with a look that said ... *please tell me I'll be alright.*

"Come on in, Mrs Diskin, please take a seat."

The friendly hospital doctor shook me by the hand and guided me to a chair opposite his. The office was just off the ward and was quite sterile in its décor; a little boxy and impersonal, even though it was airy and light. I had been in here a couple of weeks ago when Mum was first admitted. On that occasion I had sat in the other chair, over by the desk, where I did my best to give as detailed a medical history for Mum as I could. It had been hard to explain about the press, though, and how they had persecuted Mum. Some journalists would stoop so low – do anything, in fact – if it meant they could obtain a photo of Mum in this distressing condition.

"Doctor," I told the astonished medic, "it's imperative that nothing gets out concerning Mum's whereabouts. This hospital building will be inundated with snooping journalists if they find out she's here. They may even pretend to be family seeking to visit in order to reach her."

This man lived his life in the real world, a normal world. Could I really make him understand what was happening to us? Would he just think I was as sick as my Mum, exhibiting signs of paranoia? What I was relaying sounded more like a plot from a popular spy novel than real life, even to me.

"There's no need to worry, Mrs Diskin. You tell me who can visit your mother and we'll make out a permitted visitors list." He went on to confirm that no one else would be allowed in and no information would be given out unless I had been contacted first.

I'd been apprehensive back then, but Mum seemed to be improving. At least she was eating again, although one meal could take her hours to eat, because she kept slipping back to that place of nonexistence, where it seemed safer and the pain was dulled.

During her time on the ward she had 'adopted' another lady and watched out for her needs. Mum called her Susan, and indeed, I could see why. This other patient was Chinese, with eyes that tilted up at the corners just as Susan's had. Mum looked at this little lady and saw her own daughter, and this was comforting for her poor, agonized soul. She looked out for this tiny lady for most of her stay in the hospital, and no one could convince her this was not her daughter. Her mind just could not accept that Susan had died . . . it was too much pain to bear.

With my flight home to Ireland booked, I just needed an update from the doctor before leaving. It had been made clear on admission that Mum would be in this hospital for a long time to come.

"Mrs Diskin," began the doctor, "as you know, we have been doing extensive tests on your mother since she joined us to get to the bottom of why she is in this dementia. I'm afraid we've found a problem with the drainage of fluid from her brain. There is a tube that takes fluid away from the brain into the spinal column, and in your Mum's case that's not working properly."

Mum had a build-up of pressure in the brain and they needed for me, as her next of kin, to decide if they should operate to insert a shunt. The doctor went on to answer my questions as I tried to get my head around this new horror. No, this condition would not clear up on its own. No, the surgery would not correct the dementia she already had. Yes, she would always stay as lost as this, but without the operation she would certainly die from the condition as the pressure built up.

A mist wafted over me, causing a feeling of unreality. Could this really be happening? *God, I implored silently, are you serious? More? Don't I have enough worry and stress with trying to live two separate lives, keeping Barry's spirits up, visiting Mum in hospital, and wrestling with the British justice system? Do you seriously want me to take responsibility for my mother's brain, too?*

Seeing my distress, the doctor quickly added, "You don't have to decide right now, Mrs Diskin. Come back in a few weeks and let me know your decision. Nothing much will change between now and then."

This doctor, casually dressed and in his thirties, inspired confidence with his vulnerable patients. He had a trendy and approachable manner. However, this affable man was also a very learned one, so I had to accept it: Mum, as we knew her, was not coming back.

Getting the news out to friends and family about Mum's hospitalisation was not as simple as just text messaging or phoning. We knew for certain that our landline phones were tapped; indeed, Mum had had a stranger register her phone line to themselves in the same way Jill Dando had when a journalist had gained access to her private details. Our whole family had noticed the tell-tale sounds on the line that had not been there before, and it would have been unthinkable for Mum to have to suffer the humiliation of this news being cruelly broadcasted to the public. I couldn't take that chance. Worse still, if it did get out, Barry would have felt it was all his fault because he was locked up, that somehow he had caused it all. It was imperative to keep this news private, and so I sat down beside Mum in the ward's dayroom with some hastily purchased paper and some envelopes. I wrote to everyone who needed to know, using Mum's address book for reference, giving strict instructions not to mention this to anyone via phone or email correspondence. If nothing else, this would slow the bloodhounds down for a while and give us all some breathing space.

Of course, I knew I had to tell Barry something, but I didn't think it advisable to tell him everything. He needed to keep his head clear so he could work on his case. If he became agitated and worried, he would lose his concentration, and this might work against him in his legal battles. Obviously, there was no way to hide the fact that Mum was ill: she wouldn't be visiting him, and she was his most frequent visitor. The best thing to do, I thought, was to tell him only as much as was necessary, the way you might with a child. He needed as much protection as Mum.

"Barry," I told him during my next visit, "Mum won't be in for a while, she's not very well at the moment, so I'll be staying here in London for a few weeks. I'll visit you as often as I can."

"Oh no, what's wrong with her?" he asked worriedly. I really hated not being totally frank with him.

"She wasn't eating properly, honey, and now she's not well. I'll keep you informed. For now, you'll have to put up with me," I grinned.

A slow, cheeky smirk, spread across his face. "I'm not sure I can cope with that," he joked. I breathed a sigh of relief; I had successfully distracted him for a while.

From the very beginning of this nightmare ordeal, a new role seemed have been forged for me: reluctant matriarch. This was not a position that sat easily with me, and I never felt comfortable as the materfamilias, the protector of my family for Mum, Barry, my husband and the children. I wanted someone else to take over, someone more suitable than I. What did I know about the law, or the media for that matter? Was I supposed to become an expert? I'd heard stories from the US where family members had become legally trained in order to free a loved one from a wrongful conviction. I truly didn't feel up to this. Maybe if I prayed, God would give me direction. Why didn't I ask him before?

Dear Lord God, I implored. *What do you want me to do here? I feel so inadequate.*

"Stand!"

His answer, clearly spoken and heard, only added to my confusion. *Lord, I don't understand ... please tell me what I'm supposed to do!*

"Stand!" He repeated patiently. *"I want you to stand up for your brother, to stand in front of your family, and to take a stand against injustice. Just stand, my child, and I promise I will sustain you."*

A picture of Moses in Exodus 17 came to mind, holding a rod aloft during a battle. When his arms grew tired, the battle went against him. When his arms were supported, the battle was won.

Phew, I thought as I breathed a sigh of relief, little knowing just how much 'sustaining' I was going to need. A Goliath had entered our lives; now all I had to do was stand against him!

Back in Ballincollig, everyone at our church wanted an update on the events of the past few weeks. These people were, and still are, my church family. They have always been there to help with whatever was needed. When my tearful 15-year-old daughter, Carine, could not leave the house to go to school because a journalist kept trying to speak with her, it was our church family who rescued her by arriving in the minibus to collect her. They also did what they could to support us whenever I went away. My dear friend Peggy, who has since left us to be with her Saviour, called me to one side after Sunday service. "Michelle," I recall her saying, "I know it isn't much, but will you buy you and your mother a cup of coffee on me?" She handed me some Euros.

Then there was dearest Dawn: she would take charge of my youngest child, Emma-Jane. Dawn knew my concerns about being away from my daughter as she approached puberty; it caused me a great deal of pain to think Emma would not have her mother there to guide her into womanhood. Emma would alternately stay with Dawn or another close family friend, Marianne, two loving mother substitutes. My son Shane was taken under the wing of some others in the church, who took him golfing, hill climbing, and fishing. It was reassuring to know he could just hang out with guys his age, doing 'guy stuff'.

I spilled out all my worries about Mum and her prognosis during a women's Bible study morning on my return home. These wonderfully supportive women set about contacting people we knew on the prayer chain and passed on the request to the next person on their list. This special prayer request was sent far and wide . . .

"Please pray for our sister Michelle's mother, who is ill in hospital and has not been given much hope of making a full recovery. Pray God will send his healing, and will give the doctors the wisdom to best help her."

It didn't matter that most of these people would never meet us, they would pray. People in the US, France, Canada, Australia, the UK and Ireland were all praying for this unknown woman and her family. Friends and strangers alike would intercede with God on my Mother's behalf; they would pray for her full recovery and restoration. It gave us great comfort to know this.

Twelve weeks later, I returned to Charing Cross Hospital to see Mum's doctor. During all of this time I had been unable to make a decision about whether to agree to this operation on her brain. This was such a huge ask of me, and the responsibility was so overwhelming, that I was still hesitating. If I made the wrong choice, the results could be catastrophic.

After being shown into yet another sparse office, Mum's doctor launched into a discussion on Mum's response to the treatment plan to date. I listened with half an ear as my mind went over and over the repercussions of the proposed surgery. "Maybe you'd like to visit with your mum now," he suggested, getting up to indicate the end of the consultation.

"But doctor, what about the operation? We haven't discussed that yet."

He sat again, this time on the edge of his desk. "Oh, that. Mrs Diskin, your mother won't be needing surgery now. We can't explain it, but she is spontaneously recovering. She'll be able to return home in a few weeks."

Dear Lord, thank you for 'spontaneous' recovery!

5

Preliminaries

It is hard to believe that in the midst of all this turmoil, our family were having to prepare for what was to be the biggest battle of our lives.

Marilyn had engaged the services of a junior barrister, Maryam Syed, and together they had managed to secure Michael Mansfield QC, dubbed the Silver Fox by the media, to take on Barry's case. *Oh wow*, I thought. *We've secured the services of the best in the business, this is wonderful.* It was a surprise when Barry said he had never heard of him, nor his championing of human rights issues or his work with miscarriage of justice cases like The Birmingham Six and The Guildford Four. It seemed his reputation was better known in Ireland than the UK.

Mansfield's first visit to see Barry in Belmarsh caused him great concern. His client's interaction with him was very confusing.

"What is the problem here? Does he always respond like this?" he asked Marilyn.

"Oh, he's just a difficult client to deal with," she responded.

Mansfield was incredulous. "This is not just 'difficult', this is a mental health issue. I'm going to bring in a forensic psychologist, this needs to be examined further."

Professor Gísli Guðjónsson was appointed to assess Barry. His areas of expertise included clinical and forensic psychology, fitness to plead, false memory syndrome, reliability of confessions, false confessions and suggestibility in police interviews. He was joined by Doctor Susan Young, an expert in neuropsychology as well as clinical and forensic psychology, ADHD and cognitive behavioural interventions. A little later on Professor Michael Kopelman, who specialised in neuropsychiatry and memory disorders, especially amnesia, joined the team.

These three eminent doctors worked together as a forensic medical team and they were an invaluable asset to the court. Without their expertise, Barry may well have been found 'unfit to stand trial'. This was something Mansfield was seriously concerned about, because if a defendant is deemed to be unfit to stand trial, they can be hospitalised in a secure mental facility, such as Broadmoor Hospital, until they recovered sufficiently to be able to stand trial. Mansfield knew that if Barry had been put into such a hospital it would be impossible for him to recover from the disabilities he was born with. The Dando case would very quickly have disappeared and Barry would have been detained indefinitely, probably never to be released again. Everyone would have believed the case had been solved and Barry would never have had a trial, fair or otherwise.

It was during this period that Barry was finally diagnosed with a spectrum of disabling conditions, thanks to the skills of this team of professionals. Along with Attention Deficit Disorder – he was no longer hyperactive – it was found that he has Asperger's Syndrome, acquired frontal-lobe brain damage affecting his short-term memory, as well as a learning difficulty and two personality disorders. All this on top of his epilepsy. Without psychological support he would never have made it through the trial.

Professor Kopelman was very concerned for Barry and wanted to do some tests to establish if he was on the correct treatment for his epilepsy.

"Mr George was born with an abnormal brain," he told me, "and has since acquired this frontal-lobe brain damage. We have searched through all of his medical records but can find nothing to explain this injury."

Kopelman wondered if I could shed any light on this, but I couldn't. Apparently, this damage would have resulted in Barry being hospitalised, possibly unconscious.

"As to Mr George's epilepsy, I am concerned that the treatment he is on may not be suitable for the type of epilepsy he has," Kopelman explained to me. "In most people with epilepsy there is only extreme electrical activity for the duration of a seizure, but in Mr George's brain, this abnormal electrical current is active even when he has no seizures. It makes normal brain function very difficult and I'd like to do some telemetry tests to see what is going on."

Wiggling his fingers energetically to demonstrate, he went on to describe these seizures as "constant, devastating electrical currents sparking through his brain". These tests would have required a hospital stay, but Belmarsh Prison refused permission, possibly due to staffing levels. Barry would have had to be accompanied by prison staff, and would have had to be shackled to the bed, anyway, making the tests impossible due to stress.

Finally, it all made sense. Now we understood what was going on with Barry as a child. It felt like we'd found the missing jigsaw pieces. With this information, we would be able to help Barry through this ordeal – he would have support in the courtroom and he would be given techniques for dealing with his anxiety. A small victory, but one we were grateful to have achieved.

In contrast to Barry, both Mike and I were delighted that the renowned Michael Mansfield had agreed to take the case. His experience and understanding of high profile cases made him our first choice for Barry. It was our fear that Barry's chosen solicitor, though very nice, was too inexperienced to carry this case, so we'd tried all we could to get someone more experienced to represent him. Gareth Peirce, solicitor and human rights activist, agreed to take the case should Barry wish her to, but again, he had never heard of her nor knew of her track record with miscarriages of justice. Having first accepted her, he later turned her down and we were powerless to do anything about it. Legally he had the right to make his own decisions.

The first open court appearance I attended was a preliminary hearing in a lower court, Bow Street Magistrates Court. Mansfield pronounced they were going to plead 'no case to answer', since there patently wasn't any evidence against Barry. To me, this was a joy to hear, and my hopes rose until Mansfield also clarified that it would take a very brave judge indeed to throw this particular case out due to the high profile of the victim.

This was also my first experience of the media's intense interest in this case. Mike, my Aunt Betty and I arrived in the drizzling rain, having travelled there by underground. We were astounded that there were so many photographers waiting in the rain to waylay us as we entered the building. It was like reaching sanctuary when we entered the court. In retrospect, this was a just foretaste of things to come.

Barry was led in, flanked by prison guards and wearing handcuffs. What a shock we got: he was dressed in the most awful clothes imaginable. He had to hold up the filthy corduroy jeans by the waist as he walked because they were so large. Of course, no belts were allowed. The t-shirt he wore was several dirty shades of grey, but in the mist of time had probably once been white. I was horrified by his appearance. It seemed he had not been given any of his own clothing back after they were all taken away in the house searches. No one told us this and we had not been asked to buy anything for him, so the prison had supplied these dirty, ill-fitting remnants for him to wear. Of course, the media pounced on this fact.

"The defendant appeared in court today wearing dirty, stained clothing . . ."

This was the headline after the hearing. It was reported on the TV news and in the print media. They went on to describe his dishevelled appearance in detail, making it sound as though this was a choice he had made, to attend court looking like a tramp. The reporting was vitriolic, and I was determined this would never happen to him again. He was facing a murder charge, and so it suited the police for him to look like a vagrant, a deviant, a ne'er do well. They had taken every single scrap that ever belonged to him during the searches of the apartment, and now they were taking away his dignity and identity, too. They were replacing it with the one they had fabricated, one which fitted their requirements. He was so vulnerable. They had to be prevented from doing this. I didn't know how that could be achieved, but my hackles had risen and I would do all in my power to thwart them.

Having left Ireland at such short notice, there was no way I could know how long I was going to be needed in London. Therefore, I hadn't booked a return flight. It was impossible to ask my husband for more money – there simply wasn't any left. Our bank account was surviving one notch above red. I'd hoped Mum would be able to help me out, that she could arrange funds for me to get back home. Unfortunately, she was still very ill and I couldn't access her bank account, even though she'd said I should when she'd been a little more lucid. The little money I had would have to be carefully eked out. I started by using up any tinned food in Mum's store cupboard, then by buying as few provisions as possible in order to stretch my meagre budget.

These days were gruelling. First, I would travel to Belmarsh to see Barry, then I would journey back to Hammersmith and directly on to Charing Cross Hospital to visit Mum. It was my habit to visit Mum every day and Barry every second day. On the two visit days, my energy level was drained. Add to that not eating properly, and it was a real struggle just to keep going.

One evening, as I came back from one of these nine hour days bleary-eyed and hungry, I found a gift, wrapped in brown paper, waiting for me on the kitchen table. Opening it, I almost danced with joy when I saw what was contained within . . . rich juicy slabs of beef! *Alleluia!* I dined royally that night on beef steak! I gave thanks to God and offered blessings to my kindly benefactors – you know who you are. There was enough nourishing meat to last me for three days.

One reason I had run out of funds so quickly was because I didn't want Barry to appear in court wearing filthy rags again. It seemed the public were fast being fed the damaging propaganda needed for them to reach the conclusion that this man must be guilty, so I was desperately trying to keep some funds to get him something to wear. It hurt Mum and I desperately to see Barry paraded about in this way. "How can we help him, if no one will include us?" Mum asked me. We felt so out of control and impotent. It was as though Barry belonged to 'the system' now, and not to a family. We were obsolete, they were in control, and they would do with him as they pleased.

Before Mum's breakdown, we had discussed buying a new outfit for Barry to deflect further misinformation being spread by unscrupulous journalists. These people exhibited absolutely no compassion for all those caught in the crossfire. Our family were terribly offended by the suggestion that Barry was some kind of oddity or vagabond. And anyway, how did this image sit with the description given of a well-dressed man seen in Gowan Avenue around the time that Jill was killed? It seemed the police wanted it both ways, and were suggesting that this criminal mastermind dressed like a tramp most of the time, but when he wanted to kill somebody, he put on his best bib and tucker and his woollen greatcoat to carry out the crime!

With the thirty pounds I had left, I needed to buy food, rail travel to and from the prison, my flight back home, and also Barry's court suit and shoes. In short, impossible. It was definitely time for prayer.

Putting the banknotes on a table, I turned my attention to my Saviour, Jesus.

Dear Lord Jesus,

First, I come to you in praise and thanksgiving for all of the blessings you bestow upon me. I know you will always provide for my needs. I know, too, that you know the difficulties I'm facing here and I ask for your help to make the right choices.

If I buy the clothes for Barry, I won't be able to buy him shoes or buy food for myself. If I keep the money for food and train fares, I can't dress Barry for court or buy my flight home. I can't solve this predicament by myself, but I know you can. There is nothing you can't do. I put my trust firmly in you. Please, Lord, give me your wisdom and guidance.

As I prayed, this verse from the Bible came to mind:

'Trust in the Lord with all your heart, and lean not on your own understanding; in all your ways acknowledge Him, and He shall direct your paths.'
(Proverbs 3:5-6)

Finishing my prayer, I spent some quiet time reading my Bible, then went upstairs to bed and slept soundly till morning.

The next morning, the money sat there exactly as I'd left it on the coffee table, three £10 notes fanned out one on top of the other. Looking at them, I now knew what I was going to do. I would buy the clothes for Barry and I would trust God to provide for my needs. A new verse came my mind:

'Look at the birds of the air; they do not sow or reap or store away in barns, and yet your heavenly Father feeds them. Are you not much more valuable than they?'
(Matthew 6:26)

Now I knew with certainty that what I was doing was right, that God would provide for me. I could take this £30 and buy decent court clothing for Barry. That still left the absence of shoes, of course. The papers also mentioned the filthy, tattered and unlaced runners he was wearing, also not his, but at least his upper body would look presentable, and that's all that would be seen when he was seated in the dock.

Filled with God's peace now that I had decided to put myself fully in His hands, I continued to plan my day, including the all-important shopping trip. Mum's house phone rang, interrupting my thoughts.

"Michelle, it's Auntie Betty. I was worried about Barry and I wondered if I could help by buying him some clothes? I have £30 here and I can get him some new trousers or . . ."

My heart leapt with joy. Rudely butting in, I asked if she wouldn't mind purchasing some shoes with the £30. Black slip-ons, size 12, but no laces, laces are verboten! She agreed and said I could collect them later.

Alleluia, Lord, and thank you. You have provided the footwear that I couldn't afford. Thank you too, for our Aunt's generosity.

My itinerary would be very tight, but if I got back to Hammersmith by 4:30pm, I could shop in King Street then travel on by bus to see Mum in hospital before catching the number 72 bus back to East Acton. I arrived back home at around 9:30pm after a twelve hour day, exhausted but happy with what had been achieved. God had provided the money for clothes, for shoes, and He had also taken care of my hunger with prime beef . . . but He wasn't finished yet. When it came time for me to go back to Ireland, I thought I'd have to borrow money from someone to pay for the flight. *Who would I ask,* I thought, *maybe someone from church?*

Then God stepped in again. Maura arrived to Mum's house with a gift of £30, but this was not all.

"How much is your flight home, Michelle?" Maura asked. "I want to help you out if I can, since you've come over like this, leaving your own family behind in Cork."

It would cost £30 to cover my one way flight and she handed me that amount as well. Within a couple of hours, another person called by bearing a gift. Yes, another £30 in cash!

The £30 I had trustingly spent on Barry was returned to me fourfold! Now, not only could I get home to my family, but I could buy a small gift for my best friend and great supporter, Marianne.

I would also be able to buy some of those little chocolates that the children loved so much, and for Pat, a large box of Jelly Babies, his favourite.

Thirty pounds, four times over. When God provides, He does so in abundance. This was no set of coincidences, this was an example of God-incidences.

'He upholds the cause of the oppressed and gives food to the hungry. The Lord sets prisoners free.' (Psalm 146:7)

During Mum's illness, while Barry was on remand, I brought his new court clothing and shoes along to Belmarsh on my usual visit.

"What are these for? You can't bring clothing in, it all has to be posted." This was the security guard in the Visitors' Centre, but I wasn't too worried by this response. Yes, normal everyday wear *did* have to go in by post, but Marilyn had told me that there was a special category for court clothing.

"Barry has a court appearance on Monday and he doesn't have any decent clothing," I explained, knowing it was acceptable to bring these items in. "Everything he had was taken by the police."

"They should have been here last week if you wanted him to have them."

I looked at the officer, at her impassive expression, and I went on to explain that my mother was in hospital, that this was the first opportunity I'd had to get these clothes to the prison having recently arrived from Ireland. I'd had to deal with Mum's hospitalisation first.

The parcel, containing the shoes bought by Auntie Betty and the trousers and shirt that I'd worked so hard to afford, sat tantalisingly on the counter between us. So close to getting to Barry. However, as much as I pleaded, I could not move this intractable officer from her position, even though I was sure it was wrong.

Tears welled up in my eyes and spilled over, rolling down my cheeks, and I angrily dashed them away with my hand. *I must not let emotion make me weak*, I chided myself. *Barry needs me to work this out for him – don't let him down, Michelle.* But as I tried to speak, all of the stress of Mum's illness, the media's reporting of Barry's disgusting attire at the last court appearance, and the fact I was missing my own home and family so much all conspired to produce just a quivering, sobbing sound. I was undone; I had failed.

A more senior officer looking on intervened, but still to no avail. I asked him, "Please, why can't the items go through the security system the way visitors do? We have to be checked, manhandled, our clothing x-rayed, surely it would be possible for an officer to walk these items through for him? Barry can't appear in court again looking like a tramp!"

He looked at me with compassion, but he made it clear . . . Barry would not get his clothing in time for court.

Throughout these traumatic years, I have met many officers who were kindly and helpful, and who managed this without compromising security's rules and regulations. They were like an oasis in a desert; refreshing and very welcome. Unfortunately, some were legalistic and unbending, and this just heaped anguish onto already overburdened, sorrowful families.

Oh, God, I reproved. *How is this possible? After you worked everything out for us, the prison have put up a wall.* I felt confused and angry. Calming down, I understood. I thought everything rested in my strength, but it didn't. God was in control, and I had to let go and trust in him.

Okay, Father God, I know I can't get these items in, so I am leaving it in your hands. I know you can do this . . . will you, please? I can't break down this wall but you can! I prayed silently through my tears as an Angel from the Visitors' Centre came and gently led me away, producing a cup of coffee and her shoulder for crying on. My sobs eventually subsided and it was time to go in to visit Barry. I didn't tell him about the court clothes. He'd find out soon enough, and I didn't want to distress him now.

Mike and I arrived at court on the Monday morning and sat in nervous agitation awaiting Barry's entry, fearing his dishevelled appearance and the media's unfair reaction to it. The door to the dock opened and a security guard entered, closely followed by Barry and another officer. It took a moment for me to steal a look at Barry's clothing. *He was wearing his new clothes!*

Oh Lord, thank you, thank you for breaking down that wall. And thanks and blessings to the officer who acted with such compassion and integrity.

6

The Trial Collapses

February 26th, 2001

The dreaded day had arrived: the start of a trial that should never have been brought before judge and jury, a disgraceful waste of taxpayers' money on a case with no evidence. With mixed emotions, I dressed carefully in a sober, charcoal grey suit, styled my hair and applied make-up. *There, presentable enough for any formal setting.*

None of us welcomed this trial, but at least it would soon come to an end and Barry would be free.

"Breakfast is ready," Mum called up the stairs. It was so good to have her home, and so well, too. I ate the cooked breakfast that was going to become almost a ritual in our lives, then picked up my handbag, ready to dash off to the station.

"Have you remembered your Oyster card for the train, and your passport?" Mum made me check. She knew I'd need ID to enter the court, so I'd better not forget the passport. Marilyn had arranged for me to sit inside of the Old Bailey's Court One, therefore I'd have to go through security checks when I arrived.

Initially, Marilyn expected me to sit in the Public Gallery, but if I sat up there I wouldn't even be allowed to take a notepad and pen in with me. I was outraged!

"Family members aren't allowed into the court," she'd explained.

"Marilyn, Barry is disabled. He's an innocent man and this trial will affect his mental health. He must not feel abandoned to go through this alone, he needs to know I'm there with him."

"Families always sit in the Gallery, Michelle," Marilyn soothed. "They won't let you sit in the court."

"So will I be sitting with the Dando family up in the gallery?" I asked.

"Oh no, they will sit with the police in the court," Marilyn replied.

"Then I think Barry's family should sit there, too. His health may suffer if he feels he can't see me and feels he has no support. It will affect his ability to cope."

Thank goodness I had persisted. Marilyn had put a case to the court usher and as long as I behaved, I could be near him.

East Acton station is on the Central Line, so it was a direct journey through to St Paul's where I would alight. Then, it was just a few minutes' walk along Newgate Street to the historic Old Bailey, the central Criminal Court in London. Each step I took felt like the last walk of the condemned man. I was on Newgate Street, for goodness sake, where many a poor soul went before their execution! The thought made me gulp. Thank goodness Britain does not have the death penalty anymore.

Reaching the courthouse, I surveyed the waiting media throng. How would I get in without running the gauntlet of these news-hungry hounds? Shuffling myself into a crowd of legal people intent on getting into the building, I avoided the media attention, approached the security desk and presented my credentials.

"I'm sorry, miss, your name is not on our list. You'll have to go to the Public Gallery on Newgate Street," the rotund security officer directed.

Panic struck. I felt faint at the thought of being turfed back out onto the street with all those cameras waiting. As the tears poured, I stood there abject; Marilyn had obviously *not* arranged things for me. Security suggested I sit in the Gallery for today, then see what could be done for tomorrow . . . and I would have complied, really I would, except my legs would not carry me back outside to my perceived fate with the media.

"Hello, you're Barry's sister, aren't you?" A young woman appeared beside me and I looked at her in confusion. "Do you remember me? I met you and your mum at Belmarsh. All the cons in there know your Barry is innocent."

I remembered her now, her clear, coffee-coloured skin, and her ready smile. She'd been so gentle with Mum.

"My fella is up for trial today, too, but he's guilty. Your Barry shouldn't be here." This young mother, with all she had to face in life, hugged me and accompanied me out to the Gallery entrance.

"Good luck," she called as she went, leaving me safe from the media glare. I could not have been more grateful for her intervention at that time. A Godsend. Thank you for rescuing me.

After that traumatic start, all was finally sorted out. Marilyn came to the Gallery entrance and accompanied me to Court One, where I would sit from now on.

Having spent all day every day in court, I was mentally and physically shattered. We'd had the jury selection, which had gone on for days, and now the actual trial was meant to be starting. However, something else was now holding things up. On this particular day there had been in-camera discussions before Justice Gage, away from the jury. This was a debate between media representatives, who wanted to be allowed to print pictures of Barry, and the defence, who said that it would become a media feeding-frenzy if it was allowed, and that it would seriously affect the case.

At first, I managed to follow the arguments, alternately thinking that the judge had understood our concerns, then thought that he hadn't, then again that he had. The legal arguments went on and on until I fell into a kind of stupor. All I could hear was a droning sound: it just went on relentlessly. I tried to stay alert, to stay on top of things; I tried note-taking, but I kept drifting in and out. It was as though none of what was being said was real and when I woke up it would all have been just a nightmare.

The wooden benches were cold, hard, and uncomfortable. Court One of the Old Bailey was a listed building, so no changes could be made to the antiquated fixtures and fittings. Some of the other courtrooms were in the newer part of the building, and consequently had more up to date furnishings installed. Court One was very imposing, with a Dickensian atmosphere to it. Many a historic case had been tried within these hallowed walls since it was rebuilt in 1907, on the same site as the original court of 1674. Many a person had stood in the dock, awaiting justice under our adversarial system. If your case was being heard in Court One, it must be one of great importance.

The judge left to consider the arguments posed by both sides and we all waited in the court for his return. Usually we would go upstairs to the canteen for a cup of coffee and a change of scene, but at times this was too difficult for me because the Dando family were there as well. I yearned to be able to approach them and commiserate with them on their loss. They were not our enemies. They had been brought here under false pretences, too.

Of course, I could not approach them. This might have been viewed by the media as me currying favour, or being ingratiating for my brother's sake, but oh, how I longed to tell them how sorry I was for their pain.

I don't recall if they were in court on that particular day. I never felt comfortable turning to look behind me to check who was there. The Dando family and the police sat directly behind me, just to the side of the dock. My only alternative to sitting there was to sit with members of the media, and that was a horrendous thought. I would be under constant scrutiny; they would report on the smallest of actions. If I blew my nose, they would probably say I was in floods of tears. That was their way. Anyway, Barry could see me from the dock where I was sitting, and that was of paramount importance, so I took my seat every session and just braved it out.

The call went out over the public address system for everyone else to come back to Court One. The court usher made certain that everything was as it should be, then motioned to another usher,

who banged a huge ornate wooden stake twice on the floor . . .
Boom, boom.

"All rise."

Justice Gage came back in with his red, ermine-trimmed robe
swishing about him. He took his seat, adjusted his papers and his
wig, and proceeded to read out his decision. *Blah blah blah . . .*
I don't understand whatever he's telling us.

There was a hum of voices, just murmuring and shuffling sounds.
Then suddenly, people from the media seats to the left of the dock
stood up and rushed out. I'm pretty sure the judge was still saying
something about 'restraint' and 'responsible behaviour' and 'in the
public interest', but I could feel the tension in the courtroom as
they left, and I felt alarmed.

We all rose and the judge left the court. I looked around me
anxiously, and Mansfield beckoned me over while Barry was being
led away, back down to the cells to be taken back to Belmarsh.

"We lost that," he said, looking angry. "That's unfortunate.
We were really hoping the judge would keep the order in place.
This is really not good. He seems to think the media will behave
responsibly, but they won't. I am very sorry."

The legal team left to see Barry before he was taken back to
prison and I gathered up my belongings. Now it was time for my
homeward journey: back down the imposing marble staircase to
the front door, then outside, to run the gauntlet of the media
frenzy again. Steeling myself, I exited the Old Bailey and made my
way along the street. I knew that by the time I reached the corner
with Newgate Street the media hounds would abandon me and run
back to their posts outside the court building, leaving me shaken
but in peace. This is where I would take a deep breath and compose
myself before I set out on the hour-long journey back to Mum's
place and a form of refuge.

Walking along Newgate Street again, headed for St Paul's Station,
I tried to gather my thoughts as I took a few minutes to talk with
God. This was to become an important part of my days at court.

I needed this time to help reduce the extreme stress levels brought on by the media attention and by the time in the courtroom. My thoughts would be churning and I often felt punch-drunk by the end of the day. There were even days when I could scarcely put one foot in front of the other, I was so fatigued. Reaching the end of the street where the coffee vendors were open for business as usual, awaiting the influx of office workers seeking a takeaway drink for the journey, I could hear chattering and mirth as I rounded the corner and approached the station entrance. It was impossible to see my way to the top of the steps because there were so many people, all pushing and running; streaming down the stairs like water over a cliff, as though the trains would stop running in five minutes and they had to get the last one.

As I neared the steps, I caught sight of the newspaper stand to the right of the entrance, and I almost lost my footing. There, emblazoned across the front of a tabloid newspaper, displayed on the newsstand for all to see, was a full page photo of Barry. The coloured photo showed him wearing a white paper forensic suit. I could see the hood rolled up around the back of his neck. This was the coverall given to him to wear after the police had taken all his clothes away, supposedly for forensic testing, even though it had been a whole year since the crime had been committed.

This photo, the first picture allowed of the defendant in this high-profile murder case, had been released by the Met Police to a journalist, and they had done exactly what the police had wanted: printed it.

Innocent until proven guilty? Not when the police and the media collude with each other to use this type of propaganda against a defendant.

My breath caught in my throat and a myriad of emotions hit me as I stood outside of the station. Shock, horror, fear and outrage stopped me totally in my tracks. The vendor was shouting out about the first photo of Dando suspect and my heart started to pound hard in my chest. I really believed I would faint in the street as the blood rushed through my veins. It was so hard not to throw up. I stood there, transfixed by this abomination before me.

Walk, Michelle, I commanded myself. *Just get to the steps, and then you can disappear into the anonymity of the crowd. Don't faint here, for goodness sake, just keep moving.* Forcing my numbed limbs to work, I made my way down those steps and was moved along by the crowd onto the westbound platform. The trains were too crowded, so I sat on the bench and waited, letting two or three trains go by before eventually managing to board one of them. I was still in shock and my body and brain seemed to have become disconnected.

The press had free reign for the whole weekend; nothing could be done until court resumed on Monday. When Mike and I arrived at Court One, it was a very irate Michael Mansfield who met us. Incensed may be a better description.

"I *told* the judge this would happen if he lifted the restrictions on photographs of the defendant. We'll have to see what he says today."

Mansfield's usually amiable countenance had vanished, and his body language told its own tale as he paced the corridors, upper body thrust forwards, his billowing black robe flowing behind him like Batman's cape.

As I sat there nervously chewing on my lip, Mansfield called me aside again.

"I'm not sure what will happen now, but I have my doubts that this trial can continue with this jury. They could not have missed that spectacle. Anyway," he inhaled deeply, trying to calm himself, "I've been down to see Barry and he's quite stressed about it all, I just hope he can keep it all together."

Mansfield was right. The trial collapsed because of the adverse publicity caused by that picture. I had to go home to Ireland not knowing when it would be rescheduled. I was furious. Although the judge had reprimanded the press, it wasn't enough – they weren't the ones who would have to spend more time behind bars because of their irresponsible actions. My heart ached for Barry, and for the injustice of it all. It was an uneasy time as we awaited the date of the new trial.

7

The Trial: Recommencement

The trial, part two, started in earnest with a new jury on the 23rd April, 2001. Again, I was allowed to sit in the court to support Barry, for which I will always be grateful. As before, I sat in front of the police and Jill Dando's family and friends. This time the media were only allowed to use one image of the defendant in their publications, one which Mansfield had decreed that Mike and I should choose. However, *that* damage had already been done, and the genie could not be put back in the bottle.

Though I tried really hard, I found it difficult to follow all the lines of discussion and the legal points. One of the many 'in camera' discussions was about Barry's requirement for an Appropriate Adult during questioning by the police. Mansfield argued that he had not had one. The prosecution, on the other hand, said police procedures relating to the use of an Appropriate Adult had been followed. Apparently, when a vulnerable defendant is questioned, they are supposed to have someone with them who can speak for them if they get into difficulties, or if they don't understand what is being asked of them. This applies to children and mentally disabled adults in police detention to safeguard their rights under the 'Police And Criminal Evidence' (PACE) Act of 1984.

With children there needs to be an Appropriate Adult at all dealings, such as intimate searches and identification procedures. This can be a parent, guardian, social worker or trained volunteer. Unfortunately, the requirement for vulnerable adults is not so formalised and this can lead to rights not being adequately protected. The police argued that Mum was the Appropriate Adult in this case and that they had taken Barry to her home before he signed any statements. Mansfield argued she was *not* appropriate, as her own health made her vulnerable and she had not been in command of all the facts. The police had told her and Barry that he was only helping them with their enquiries, which is a very different prospect to being a suspect in the case. She would not have understood the danger to Barry and would not have been on her guard, probably thinking that a small discrepancy by the police wouldn't matter much.

Being new to the world of all things legal, I thought an Appropriate Adult would be appropriate to the needs of the defendant, like a translator for languages or a sign language interpreter for the deaf, but apparently not. Anyone deemed responsible by the police, as long as it was not an officer or someone working for the police, could be used. In court, the police showed a video of their interviews with Barry in custody. His solicitor was present, with a social worker as the Appropriate Adult, someone who didn't know Barry. It was clear neither of them understood his complex mental health needs. They didn't speak up for him when the police were badgering him repetitively, even though he had already answered the same question many times. In these overwhelming circumstances, this mentally disabled man had to fend for himself as he fought to show his innocence. The system had let him down again; there was no protection for his vulnerability.

On and on the arguments went.

"We will need to call Mrs George into court so the court can decide if she is mentally competent to be the Appropriate Adult for Mr George," the prosecutor, Orlando Pownall, declared.

Barry was so upset at the prospect of his poor mother being subjected to this ignominy, displayed for the world through the unforgiving media coverage that he refused to allow it despite it being in his best interests to do so. He would not expose his mother to more pain. She would not have to stand in the witness box and show what affect her strokes and her subsequent breakdown had had on her: the slurring of her words, her vagueness.

For me, watching Barry with his frightened expression being taken down to the cells between sessions broke my heart. The feeling of being completely out of control was acute; we had no say over what happened to Barry during this time, he belonged to *them* now. We could not protect him.

The following day in court, the prosecution declared that if Barry needed a team of doctors to say he could not take the stand to give evidence, then they wanted to assess him, too. Mansfield believed that Barry would not manage to give evidence on his own behalf due to his communication problems. The prosecutor, with his superior intellect, could have run rings around Barry as he struggled in front of a jury who had no understanding of his complex difficulties. While Barry would still be trying to get his point across to question one, Pownall would be posing the fifth. *Are you being evasive, Mr George, refusing to answer my questions?* That was our fear, that Pownall would overwhelm him using his own exceptional intelligence against Barry's disabilities.

Dr Caroline Logan was the clinical psychologist engaged by the prosecution, and she was given access to Barry down in the cells of the Old Bailey. There was to be a trial within a trial away from the jury. As the law stands, a defendant who decides not to give evidence can have inference drawn from it that they have something to hide, an inference of guilt. Mansfield argued that in the case of a disability no inference should be taken. The prosecution wanted to prove Barry was capable of answering questions to disprove his defence of having communication disabilities.

Dr Logan went down to see Barry and we all went up to the canteen for a coffee to await the call back to court. The next I heard was that the guards on duty by the cells had reported being very concerned. Dr Logan was shouting at Barry in the cell. She could be heard through the door and along the passageway, bullying him, trying to elicit a response. We were summarily called back to court, where Dr Logan explained that she had diagnosed multiple personality disorders, now outlined in her report. The judge then asked her to justify her behaviour with the defendant. When she couldn't, he reprimanded her and discredited her report.

Dr Logan's findings were not used by the court, but later they *were* leaked to the media who used this report to make Barry seem like the monster they'd been portraying him to be. The fact this report had been discredited by the court never reached the public's ear.

Sitting with others in the canteen one morning, I mentioned that I would really like to send a Bible verse to Barry to help keep his spirits up. I knew he had his Bible with him – after all, the media had mocked him enough for carrying it – so I knew he'd be able to look up the references I sent.

> *"Be strong and courageous. Do not be afraid or terrified because of them, for the LORD your God goes with you; he will never leave you nor forsake you."*
> *(Deuteronomy 31:6)*

I also sent:

> *"The LORD is my light and my salvation – whom shall I fear? The LORD is the stronghold of my life – of whom shall I be afraid?*
> *(Psalm 27:1)*

Imagine my surprise when I received a Bible verse back from Barry, one perfectly suited to what *I* was going through!

> *"May the God of hope fill you will all joy and peace as you trust in him, so that you may overflow with hope by the power of the Holy Spirit."*
> *(Romans 15:13)*

I'd underestimated Barry; he knew his Bible better than I'd realised. Of course, he had been studying the Bible in readiness to take his Believer's Baptism at the time the police arrested him.

The strain on Barry during the trial was huge. Every day, he had to listen to a barrage of accusations and misinterpretations, hence Dr Young was called upon to teach him anxiety management and relaxation techniques so that this trial didn't break down, too.

Initially, Dr Young was to sit next to Barry in the dock for all of the proceedings, but after the prosecution expressed their objection to seeing Barry in the dock with a good-looking blonde woman, Dr Young moved to the body of the court when in the presence of the jury and monitored Barry from there. Mansfield believed the prosecution were concerned because Jill Dando had also been a good-looking blonde woman, and they feared it may sway the jury in Barry's favour.

Dr Young met with Barry at each break to provide anxiety management interventions and to assess his understanding of the proceedings. These interventions were important because anxiety exacerbates the likelihood of seizures, which might go unnoticed by everyone else because of their type, Absence Seizures.

During a particularly arduous period, Barry became very ill in the cells and Dr Young and the team were called to go to him. When they came back up to the canteen I was shocked to learn that he was suffering from Psychogenic Blindness. This meant that his optic nerves were working, but he could not see. This psychological disorder was brought on by unbearable stress. Surely killing someone would be a lot more stressful than standing trial? If he'd killed Jill Dando he could never have coped for a whole year and evaded capture, without cracking up.

The blindness did not ease, and Barry had to go back to Belmarsh, where he suffered prison guards and fellow prisoners thrusting things into his path which he bumped into or fell over. They did not believe his symptoms. It was not until the following week, when Dr Gisli Guðjónsson worked with Barry using hypnosis that his sight returned. Of course, the press didn't believe Barry was really ill either, and they had a field day mocking him, as did the police and the prosecution. I overheard them in the public corridor laughing and referring to him as 'The Afflicted'.

Five weeks after the recommencement of Barry's trial, another high profile case started, this one allocated to Court Two. The Honourable Jeffrey Archer, Baron of Western-super-Mare, Life Peer, ex-MP and celebrated author was on trial for perjury. Mansfield informed me of this when taking a few minutes to chat between sessions as he always tried to do, keeping me in the loop. Surprisingly, and kindly, he was not just concerned for Barry, but for me, also.

"Rumour around the court is that Archer is peeved because Barry has Court One. He's also decided he's not going to take the stand in his trial, having heard that Barry won't be. It won't sit well with the judge, I can tell you. Barry is disabled and that's why we don't want him on the stand, but Archer thinks it sets a precedent for him . . ."

Archer, who'd had a chequered career, had taken a case against The Daily Star in 1987 because they'd said he'd paid a prostitute a sum of money for sex. He'd won £500,000 in damages, but now he was back in court charged with perjury. I'd watched his wife, Mary, a poised and elegant woman, who wore her sophistication as a shield against the vulnerability of exposure to the press. She struggled as I did to get into the courthouse each day, and I'd witnessed her battle against wind, rain and umbrellas. We were both nearing the entrance from opposite directions when I saw her raise a hand to push back her perfectly coiffed and bobbed hair so she could see where she was going. The next day on the front page of newspapers was a photo of her with the caption 'Mary poses for cameras'. She wore a fraught expression, which reinforced my decision never to give them a photo opportunity, never to show my emotions.

Surprisingly, I was to find there were other parallels between Jeffrey Archer and ourselves. He and Barry share the same birth date, 15th April, though Archer is fifteen years older. Both spent time in Belmarsh at the same time, where Archer wrote his Prison

Diaries series, telling the world that no one believed Barry George was guilty, although he seems to have talked of Barry's conviction before it had actually happened! Nothing, though, could top this conversation with Mansfield for bizarre goings on.

"Michelle, there is something very strange going on in the Archer case. The police are carrying out investigations to see if he might have had something to do with Jill Dando's death. They think Archer may have ordered a hitman to kill his secretary, Angela Peppiatt." Mansfield related this to me during a break in the court's proceedings. Noting my quizzical expression, he explained further. "She's giving incriminating evidence against him in this trial. Jill may have been killed because she was blonde, like Peppiatt. They lived in the same area, and they both drove similar blue BMW cars."

"What?!"

Everything started to whirl around in my head, making it difficult to form coherent thoughts. I'd always enjoyed the novels by Jeffrey Archer, with all of their political twists and turns, but now it felt like we were bit players in his latest novel, caught up and blown about like chaff in his frenetic saga. Eventually the light-headedness lifted, settling down to mere disbelief that this was happening. Would it help us? Was it possible? Then, the realisation hit me.

"Michael, do you mean that the police are investigating Archer for the murder of Jill Dando while they are simultaneously trying to convict Barry of it? How is that even legal? This has to show they don't really believe Barry did this. If they were one hundred percent certain they had their killer in Barry, they would not be looking at Archer. They *know* Barry is innocent!"

The duplicity made me reel. Our lives had been thrown into turmoil, yet they knew Barry didn't do this. How could the police be in one courtroom trying to convince a jury of a defendant's guilt, whilst believing the killer may be someone in another courtroom in the same building? Where was the great British justice that I'd believed and trusted in? It all left me painfully disillusioned; it felt like a stab in the back.

Mansfield felt there was nothing we could do about it at the time. We just had to let it play out.

Running the gauntlet of the media four times a day was agonising for me, and was something I would never get used to. Friends tried to make light of it by talking about my celebrity status, but this was not glitz and glam: I had a job to do, an important one. Mum could not go to court because she was much too fragile. The media alone would have been enough to send her back to hospital, without being subjected to all the lies being told about her son in a court of law! No, she had to stay away: go out shopping, visit friends, anything other than sit at home all day. Mike was in court when he could get time off from work in Limerick, though he mostly travelled in on his own, getting to the Old Bailey very early to miss the media scrum that would ensue. It was good to have someone else in the building with me on those days, but they were few, and it was the loneliest feeling sitting in the court or the canteen alone, with only the occasional coffee-time companion or the unwanted intrusion of a journalist to keep me company.

The overwhelming pressure came to a head one day when I was about to leave the court to go home. I found I could not walk; my legs refused to do as I told them. There I stood inside the main door wringing my hands together, too terrified to leave.

God, I silently prayed, *you have to help me. I can't face that outrageous mob again, I just can't.*

Panic had seized me. The prospect of the news-hungry hounds shouting at me . . . "Michelle, over here Michelle!" or, "Look this way, tell us how you feel." They jostled for position right in front of my feet: I'd tried walking faster to get away but that didn't help, they had guides who would run forwards and grip the belts of the camera operators from behind, enabling them to run backwards in safety. Their intrusive cameras were just inches from my face. I knew that a photograph of my pain would have added seasoning to their news coverage, but I would not give them any emotion to further exploit us.

Oh, Lord, tell me what to do. I can't stay here, but I can't go out there, either. Then, I heard Him.

"My daughter, are you a follower of Christ?"

Yes, Lord, I replied in my confusion.

"Then know, if you follow, Jesus must go before you. See . . . the hem of his gown."

Yes! There it was, the hem of the robe of Jesus, swishing just ahead of me. I could see his sandal underneath as he walked. Now I could go anywhere. The vicious mob could not crowd me; there was an invisible force field around me that they could not break through.

God had given me a vision that day to comfort me. I just had to keep following Jesus.

It was during this daunting mid-trial period that I met Paddy Hill for the first time. Paddy was one of the six men wrongly convicted of the Birmingham pub bombings. He was following the news reports of the trial of Barry George from his home in Scotland. Paddy Hill had set up the Miscarriages of Justice Organisation (MOJO), with help from John McManus, after Paddy had been exonerated of that terrible crime. He wanted to direct other miscarriage of justice victims on their journey to overturning their wrongful convictions.

As he watched, his heart was touched by the sight of a lone woman walking in and out of court every day, assailed by news crews. He had heard enough of the evidence to believe a miscarriage of justice was about to take place but he could only help after conviction, not before, and then only if the defendant asked for his help. However, something struck Paddy about this case and that sad lonely figure on the screen and he came down to London.

"Get in there and support that poor woman," he told one of his volunteer workers, Ann. "She's all on her own."

Paddy, who had himself had such traumatic times in British courts, could not bring himself to enter the building. Instead, he prowled about in the street outside the Old Bailey, pacing back and forth, smoking cigarette after cigarette and telling the waiting journalists, in technicolour language, exactly what he thought of the proceedings taking place in Court One.

Ann, also known as Moneypenny after the James Bond stories, approached me during a break from proceedings while I was in the canteen having coffee with Mike.

"Hello there. My name's Ann, and I've been asked to have a chat with you to see if we can help you at all."

Looking up at this slim, fifty-something woman with a very short blonde hairstyle, severe black dress and with a mother-of-pearl crucifix hanging at the demure neckline, it's no wonder that my overloaded brain thought she was a nun in civvies! Laughing out loud at this, she quickly disabused me of that notion: she told me she worked with MOJO and that Paddy had sent her in.

That was my first encounter with the organisation that has remained a part of my life to this day, one where it has been my privilege to meet many more wrongly convicted and badly damaged people, now freed and trying to integrate back into a society that can never truly understand the trauma they have been through.

8

The Trial: Witness Evidence

The facts of the case as presented to the jury were that on the 26th April 1999, much loved TV presenter Jill Dando was murdered as she approached her own front door in Gowan Avenue, Fulham, South West London. She had taken the keys out of her handbag, but had not opened the door when she was grabbed from behind. Fresh bruises on her right forearm indicated she had been gripped there, then forced down to the step. Ms Dando was then was shot through the head once from behind the left ear. There were no fingerprints or DNA at the scene and no murder weapon has ever been found.

Several people came forward to say they had seen a man in the street on the day of the murder and were interviewed by the police, though some were not interviewed until a year later. These sightings can be summarised thus: a man of between 5'8" and 6' tall, between the ages of 30 and 40. He was described as being of stocky build, but also medium or skinny. He had a Mediterranean appearance, or was variously portrayed as having olive, pink, and white skin. His hair was dark, dark brown, or blonde. It was collar length, but was also said to be short, or long and floppy, and was swept back. This man was said to be wearing a dark suit, a dark blue suit, or a grey or black suit with a white shirt, light blue shirt, open-necked shirt, and also a blue tie or a red tie.

At 7:00am the man was described as clean shaven, but by 9:30am he was like 'Desperate Dan' the comic-book character with a five o'clock shadow. He was further described as smartly dressed, but untidy; not like a chauffeur but like a mini-cab driver, and not 'city smart' but like an estate agent. He wore a Barbour style jacket ending at the hip, a three-quarter length wax coat to mid-thigh, a dark Crombie style woollen coat, or no coat. At times, it was said he had been seen carrying a mobile phone. The man observed leaving the scene of the murder was considered calm, but the man at the bus stop was sweating profusely.

In the first sighting of a man at 7:00, he was said to be standing beside a double-parked maroon-coloured saloon car outside of No. 28 and across the road from Jill's home. The witness, Ms Susan Mayes, in her statement to the police described the man she saw as being of Mediterranean appearance with olive skin, clean shaven and with collar-length dark hair which was swept back. He wore a dark-coloured suit and an open-necked white shirt and seemed slightly overweight and untidy.

"He appeared to be waiting for something," Ms Mayes told the court. "I thought he was too scruffy to be a chauffeur, so he must be a mini-cab driver. He didn't like me looking at him and tried to hide his face."

A typical springtime morning, the day was wet, grey and drizzly, and the witness was hurrying along on her way to work with her umbrella over her head. Peering out from under it, she saw the man wipe the windscreen of the car 'as if to clear it', using his hand and not a cloth.

"I thought this was strange behaviour," said Ms Mayes in her testimony from the witness box, "so I looked at him again."

"How long in total did you look at the man?" Mansfield asked.

"About 6 seconds."

Sixteen months after the crime, this witness attended an identity parade where she picked out Barry. Then, at the first trial, she did a dock-identification, causing a great deal of consternation because this is not acceptable under British law. She pointed to Barry and said . . . "It was the defendant I saw!" The jury were immediately told to dismiss this, but the damage it did in its shocking nature could not be underestimated.

Another neighbour, who was in the street a few minutes later, did not see a double-parked car or a man in the street even though, as she testified in court, she was carefully watching up and down the street as she loaded boxes into the boot of her car.

"I needed to be sure it was safe to leave the house door and the car boot door open as I moved back and forth with my boxes. I think I would have noticed a double-parked car in the street."

Between 9 and 9:30 that same morning, a man was seen walking along Gowan Avenue from Munster Road. As he crossed the road over to Jill's side of the street, two women who were looking out of an upstairs bedroom window noticed him. They described him as wearing a dark blue or grey suit, a white or light blue shirt, and a red or blue tie. Each of them remembered him differently.

Mrs Stella de Rosney said he was smartly dressed, but her daughter-in-law Mrs Charlotte de Rosney disagreed.

"No, he looked more like an estate agent, not quite 'city smart'." Charlotte de Rosney also described him as having a 'Desperate Dan' look.

A year after the killing, on 26th April 2000, Miss Belinda Normanton came forward to the police after hearing the Crimewatch appeal for information. She said she had seen a man in the street at around 9 or 9:30 the previous year as she walked to her embroidery class. She spoke of a man walking along the street, carrying a mobile phone and wearing a bracelet or a watch on his other hand. He had dark hair and was wearing a dark suit, a white open-necked shirt and no tie.

Ms Dando's next door neighbour, Mr Richard Hughes, heard Jill activate her car lock at around 11:35. It emitted a chirping sound, which he recognised because it was the same make and model as his wife's car. A couple of moments after hearing the lock, he heard a short scream.

"It sounded like Jill was surprised by someone," Mr Hughes said in his statement to the police. "I looked out of the upstairs window but I couldn't see Jill lying on the pathway."

He did, however, hear the gate click and saw a man carrying a mobile phone walking briskly away towards Fulham Palace Road. This is in the opposite direction from Barry's home.

Simultaneously, another neighbour from across the street, retired naval officer Mr Geoffrey Upfill-Brown, was at his own gate. He had just come home from buying groceries when he spotted a man moving very quickly away from the vicinity of Jill's gate. When the man noticed he'd been seen, he slowed down to a brisk walk and continued on until he became obscured by a parked lorry. This neighbour also didn't see Jill's body lying at her doorstep. Jill's body was not discovered until 11:40 by a shocked passer-by who alerted the authorities. The two neighbours' description of the man differed in that Mr Hughes says the man was wearing a Barbour-style waxed jacket and had dark collar-length hair, heavier on top. Mr Upfill-Brown was adamant that the man had dark, floppy hair, very much longer, and wore a different style of jacket. It is accepted that they both saw the same person.

Gowan Avenue is a busy thoroughfare for pedestrians and it is the most direct walking route linking Munster Road with Fulham Palace Road. A Victorian terraced street, it is in an exclusive part of Fulham. This is not a quiet cul-de-sac and it has many businesses and offices nearby. Also, being within walking distance of major public transport lines into the City, this street would be busy with all sorts of people going to places of work between 7:00 and 9:30. Mansfield pointed out that seeing a man of average height in a dark suit could hardly have been said to be exceptional, rather, it would be the norm.

Pownall pronounced: "There is a unity of appearance. It is inconceivable it was anyone but the defendant, Barry George."

In 1999, the year Jill was murdered, Barry was 39 years old. Above average in height, he was beginning to thicken around the waist.

His dark hair was cut with an unattractive short-back-and-sides appearance. Barry's barber of five years, Mr George Lazou, was traced and interviewed in 2002 for the 'Cutting Edge' Documentary programme on Channel 4, 'Did Barry George Kill Jill Dando?' one of the documentaries exploring the evidence against Barry. Barry had asked his solicitor at the time of the trial to do this but she had declined, explaining, 'There is no funding allocated for the defence to carry out investigations because the defendant has nothing to prove.'

During the documentary, Mr Lazou stated:

"I didn't like cutting his hair that short up the back of his neck, level with his ears." He drew an imaginary line on the back of a customer's head, from earlobe to earlobe, to demonstrate. "Other customers could see it and it looked all wrong but I couldn't persuade him to change it."

"So, could Barry's hair have been described as collar length in 1999?" queried James Cohen, who produced the programme and carried out the interviews.

"Nah, no way!" Eli, the other barber, replied.

"Shoulder length, then?"

"Nah, not at all."

"Long and straight maybe?"

"Nope." The barber shook his head again and gave a rueful smile.

"Well then, long and curly?"

Ceasing to cut the head in front of him in the barber's chair, he turned to the camera and responded, "Nah, I never could understand how they said that was George. He never looked like that!"

A year after the murder, and after Barry had been charged with the killing, Mr Hughes and some other witnesses were asked to attend a conventional line-up. This meant they would view the people on the line-up through a two-way mirror. They had the opportunity for a close inspection of the nine men. Mr Hughes didn't pick out Barry. In fact, he didn't pick out anyone. Three others, who also attended this line up but were not called as witnesses, didn't pick anyone out either.

Mr Upfill-Brown and the four female witnesses later attended a video ID, a similar procedure to that now used by the Met Police and throughout the UK. This was because Barry, having been in one conventional line-up and not having been picked out, declined to go to further parades, as was his right. He explained that every time he left Belmarsh he had to endure a strip and cavity search before leaving the prison, and again on his return. He reasoned that if the witnesses at the time and scene of the crime did not pick him out as the killer, why should he go through all of the ignominy of the searches just so the police can ask people who were *not* present at the time or scene of the crime to try and identify him?

The video ID method used in the Dando case was a series of cameo type images, face forward, which was viewed by the witnesses in the presence of an officer as well as Marilyn Etienne. Nine images were presented for viewing in DVD format on a TV screen at the police station. Each witness was asked, after viewing the recording twice, if they could pick out the man they saw in the street that day.

"You can ask to view them all again, or just some, if you so wish," the officer informed each witness. As each cameo was accompanied by a number, he or she should identify using that number. For example: I recognise number 9 as the person I saw in the street that day.

Mr Upfill-Brown, who saw the man leaving the scene of the crime, didn't identify anyone. In court we watched the police recordings on TV monitors set up for the trial, showing the witnesses being asked if they could identify a person from the video. I was shocked to learn that even though witnesses said they were not sure, this was considered as evidence against a murder suspect in a court of law in England.

"It might have been number 5, but I'm not sure," said one.

"It could be number 2, but it could also be number 5 or number 8 and I think number 9," said another.

Only one person made a positive identification. After some humming and hawing over her answer, she eventually picked out number 2, which was the position allocated to Barry. This was the witness from 7:00 in the morning, four and a half hours before the crime took place. The other three witnesses, from 9 to 9:30am, over two hours before the crime, were not able to make a positive identification.

Charlotte de Rosney said she thought number 2 was familiar, but was not sure it was the man in the street that day. Number 8 was also a contender.

Stella de Rosney looked at numbers 2, 5, and 8 but did not make a positive identification. She was looking for pinky skin, she said, but they all looked grey.

Ms Normanton thought she'd seen number 2 but the beard made it difficult to be sure.

Since Barry spent his days roaming about the streets in this neighbourhood, visiting shops, businesses and cafés, it would not be strange to find him familiar-looking, especially as three of these witnesses admitted to buying groceries in the same local food store. Barry was a regular presence in the area. In fact, one of the other people viewing that day, the postman, said he recognised Barry but not as the person he had seen in the street on the 26th April 1999.

Professor Tim Valentine, an expert in this field, had analysed the eyewitness evidence for the 'Cutting Edge' TV documentary about Barry's conviction. He explained that at a video ID, the suspect should be moved around to different numbered positions after each witness has viewed the line-up. This procedure would rule out any possible influence from communication between witnesses or police staff who were present when a previous identification had been made. Apparently, the police followed the correct procedure at this stage and took the appropriate precautions to stop witnesses who have seen the line-up from talking to other witnesses who had not yet viewed it.

Professor Valentine also clarified something for me which I had been totally ignorant of before, because I had not had access to case papers. He said the identifications officer offered to use a video with Barry at a different position after each witness, but that Barry's solicitor had chosen to continue with him at the same position, number 2, throughout. This decision had important consequences when the witnesses later discussed their experience.

The following scenario could not have taken place if Barry's solicitor had accepted the offer to move the cameo pictures around to various slots. Three of the witnesses were asked to wait in a room at Hammersmith Police Station after viewing the video ID and were told they would be driven home by an officer. They were allowed to speak with each other and were all driven home in the same vehicle. This is completely against police procedure. ID witnesses are not supposed to meet up, and they are certainly not supposed to discuss the participants of the line-up with anyone else. This group of witnesses conceded, under cross examination by Mansfield, that they did just this in the back of the car, and within the hearing of the driver, PC Bartlett.

"Who did you pick?" asked Ms Mayes, continuing quickly, "I picked out the right man, I picked out number 2." This was the witness from 7:00am.

When witnesses have completed their identification task, they should not know whether they are right or wrong, but this witness was confident she had picked the right man. How could she have felt so confident of this? It was because only Ms Mayes had a statement taken by the police after the identification procedure. The others, who had not made a positive ID, did not, prompting one of the other witnesses to observe that it was 'obvious' that Susan Mayes had made the 'right' identification.

The conversation in the car continued. "Well, I looked at number 2 as well, and I thought it was him but I couldn't be quite sure. Now I realise I was correct."

"Oh, so did I!" Now both of the other women felt strengthened in their non-identifications.

This type of discussion between witnesses is not acceptable practice, but it was allowed as evidence in the trial against Barry

George. What made the case of Regina v George so different? It had to be the profile of the victim. Mansfield said that if the killer of someone as famous as Jill Dando could not be found a year after her murder, then other journalists, celebrities and the general public could not feel safe anymore. This crime had to be seen to be solved to appease the public.

One of these witnesses subsequently went on to have an affair with the police officer who drove them all home that day, PC Bartlett, and they continued to have this affair while the case progressed to trial. Charlotte de Rosney was still called by the prosecution to give evidence in court even though she should have been excluded, because her evidence could have been compromised by possible pillow talk. Another example of the law being influenced by the victim's profile. In the words of Mansfield, "Number 2 will do."

"So, PC Bartlett, can you tell us, was there an explanation as to why these witnesses were driven home in the same vehicle, when it is clearly against police procedure?" Mansfield glanced around the courtroom with an incredulous look as he cross-examined the officer in court.

"Yes. It was to save money."

On the morning of the murder, Barry awoke, got dressed, picked up a plastic supermarket bag loaded with documents and assorted pieces of paper and made his way on foot to Hammersmith and Fulham Action on Disability (HAFAD), a centre set up to aid people who need assistance with a variety of health and social related information. The office was located on Greswell Street, just off Fulham Palace Road.

Arriving without an appointment, Barry was told he could not be seen without one, as this rule was strictly adhered to. Barry, being Barry, resisted this decision and became somewhat agitated.

"I really need help with this today, it's to do with my housing. I'm here now, and I have all of my papers with me. It doesn't make sense for me to come back tomorrow, surely someone can see me, please?"

He continued on, speaking about the problems he was having with a GP and about a legal issue to do with a cycling accident as well. This was not unusual behaviour for Barry. As part of his disability, he could not understand that his needs were not always immediate. If he needed something, then he needed it now! He would persist in seeking to have what he wanted and would use any verbal means to express his upset if thwarted. Appointments and rules just got in the way of him getting his problems sorted. Also, having an impaired short-term memory due to brain damage, he was likely to forget to attend to these documents if he didn't do it right away, falling foul of bureaucracy because he was late returning forms. By Barry's logic, he had assembled everything he needed in this untidy, overflowing bag, he had arrived at the office and he wanted to be seen.

The first person he met at the HAFAD office was the administrator, Rosario Torres. Nobody was seen without an appointment at this centre and she was not going to back down on this decision. She told Barry he would have to make an appointment for the following day. Calling on case worker Susan Bicknell, who Ms Torres testified was 'sitting having a tea break in another room', she asked Mrs Bicknell to make the arrangements and then went back to her own desk. She continued to monitor Barry as he sat cooling his heels on a bench in the waiting area. His breathing was laboured and heavy and his face was florid. He was stimming; his legs keeping up a rhythmic trembling, causing his knees to bounce up and down, and he wore a worried expression. She could see he was upset and two other women working in the centre also noted his arrival and his demeanour.

"Please, I just need some help with this, can't you see me now?" Barry protested. "Why do I need to walk all the way back again tomorrow?"

Mrs Bicknell was in a new job with HAFAD and this was her first day. Jotting down the time she started to speak with her client as

11:50, she began asking him questions to ascertain his needs, taking further notes from him so she would recall what was required. She then gave him an appointment for the following day. This was a procedure Mrs Bicknell was unused to. In her previous positions working with people with disabilities, she would have dealt with the client immediately if she had the time, but she felt it best to comply. After all, she was the new girl here and she didn't think it advisable to make waves on her first day.

In fact, she didn't have any appointments on her list for that day and could have seen to Barry's needs there and then, saving them both the need to do this twice. In the witness box, Mrs Bicknell testified that Barry had been passed over to her at 11:50 and was speaking with her for approximately fifteen minutes. He had been speaking with the other member of staff for a quite a few minutes also, so had arrived at the centre much earlier than that. She testified that he was wearing a yellow top and blue jeans and was carrying an untidy plastic carrier bag full of papers tucked under his arm.

Barry didn't make it to his appointment with Mrs Bicknell the next day at HAFAD. The whole of Fulham, indeed the rest of Britain, was buzzing with the awful news of Jill's death and the speculation that always surrounds these terrible and shattering events. Barry got caught up in it all. He probably felt a personal connection to it, since it had happened in the vicinity of his home. He went around the area asking businesses and shops to sign cards of condolence. It would never have occurred to him that other people would view this as odd behaviour. Feeling the collective pain of mourning in Fulham, he would have wanted to show what he considered to be due respect and the sharing of community grief.

Two days after the killing, on the 28th April, Barry retraced his steps and returned to HAFAD and to Traffic Cars, the taxi company that had given him a free ride at 1pm on the day of the murder. He was concerned that he may become a suspect to the police for this killing and wanted to check out his times with them, also checking that they remembered him. This was what the police referred to as him 'concocting an alibi', but this was normal behaviour for this mentally disabled man, who was so frequently stopped by the police in the street. Normal behaviour, too, for a man who has no true concept of time as part of the myriad mental disabilities he was born with. Barry knew he would not be able to recall the details of that momentous day and that, as one of the local characters in Fulham, the police would be likely to want to speak with him.

This was not paranoia. Barry had been pulled in by the police for the 1992 murder of Rachel Nickell, before the police and the Criminal Profiler Paul Britton set their nets for Colin Stagg. Then *Stagg* was almost railroaded to conviction. At the time of Jill Dando's death, Stagg was still living under a cloud of suspicion after the judge at the trial in August 1993 threw the case out because the police had employed the use of a honey-trap, a female undercover police officer, to befriend him, offer to sleep with him, and try to lead him into confessing.

Stagg was not publicly exonerated until December 2008 after serial killer Robert Napper pleaded guilty to manslaughter, due to diminished responsibility. Napper might well have been caught earlier had the police not set their sights exclusively for Stagg, to the detriment of all other evidence. They refused to see the link between two appalling murders, even though the killings were clearly similar. Since the police had spoken to Barry about the Rachel Nickell murder, it was no stretch of the imagination to think they would question him about a high profile killing that took place in his neighbourhood. Barry has an unhappy knack of always looking furtive and guilty, and an ability to attract attention to himself.

9

The Trial: Additional Evidence

Regina v George. That's what was printed on the spines of the lever arch files that lined the wall in front of the dock. They were stacked in cardboard cases, six folders to each, eight boxes across and five high.

"Michael," I asked incredulously, "are all those files about Barry? What on earth is in them?"

"They contain every detail of all aspects of this case. Jill Dando's life, old boyfriends, family, friends, history, case notes of the investigation, other suspects. None of those files has anything to do with Barry. They belong to the prosecution."

My thoughts turned to the trollies I'd seen, laden down with boxes of files, being wheeled past the media in the street and into court. The legal juniors pushing and pulling them always seemed to struggle under their load. All were labelled Regina v George. They were multiple copies of the same files. One for each person on the prosecution team. Did the media hounds know that, or did they believe that they all related to Barry George? Did they even care what the truth was?

"Michael, that's terrible! They're right in the jury's line of sight, they can't miss them. They'll think Barry must be a serial killer, or career criminal. Won't that prejudice the case? Influence the jury? Why are they there?"

"They don't need to be, Michelle, and they won't be referred to."

So they were window dressing for the jury and the media. Whatever happened to the presumption of innocence, or the right to a fair trial? This case was, quite literally, stacked against us.

The additional evidence in this case consisted of:

- 800 hoarded magazine and newspaper publications, including copies the BBC's Ariel, a magazine for staff
- An interest in celebrities
- One hundred undeveloped rolls of 35mm film
- Lying to the police
- An 'unhealthy' interest in guns
- A particle of firearms discharge residue (FDR) found on Barry's coat
- A single cloth fibre

The police discovered that eight of the eight hundred publications seized during searches of Barry's flat contained pictures of Jill Dando before her death. One percent. The police said this proved his obsession with Jill Dando. Barry had stacked this mountain of printed material against one wall of his chaotic flat. On another wall he had stockpiled empty pizza boxes, in true hoarder style. Not one photo was circled, cut out or otherwise marked or highlighted. At trial, Mansfield, in a throw away comment, asked, "I wonder how many of those eight hundred publications contained articles about Manchester United? Because there was certainly more likelihood from that pile of papers of an obsession with that team than there ever was with Jill Dando!"

As to the obsession with celebrity, the whole of the western world is obsessed with it. That is why we have so many reality TV shows, celebrity lifestyle magazines, awards ceremonies and more. The only celebrities Barry had an interest in were male music performers or stuntmen in films that he would have liked to emulate.

Much was also made of the one hundred rolls of undeveloped 35mm film found scattered amongst Barry's belongings. This, too, was seen as proof that he had killed Ms Dando. The films contained many subjects, as well as images of women he had seen in the street. Some had been taken with permission and some covertly. Not one image had ever been viewed by Barry . . . they were *undeveloped*. He was not at home poring over them night after night, salivating, which was the implication by the prosecution at trial and by the media. He had never seen them.

Neither had he set eyes on a photo of someone in a gas mask and holding a broken gun. To this day Barry believes it wasn't him in that photo, but a friend of his. The photo had been taken in the eighties and lay undisturbed and undeveloped until the year 2000, when the police found the roll.

"Have you ever seen this photograph, Mr George? This is you, isn't it?" The interviewing officer asked this of Barry over and over during interrogation. Barry has a defective memory, but the police took his refusal to say he had seen this image as a lie. Neither his Appropriate Adult nor his solicitor had intervened.

Lies. Another plank of evidence relied upon by the prosecution. Pownall said Barry had lied about knowing Jill and about being obsessed with her, he'd lied to the police when being questioned in custody, and he had also lied in an effort to create a false alibi. It was also put to Barry that he had lied about owning a gun. In the 80s, he had owned a replica gun that fired plastic pellets and a blank firing gun, a starter pistol with the barrel filled in. They were stolen from him by some young friends who lived in the same flats as him, and he had never replaced them. A witness from the same housing project related in court that Barry had come to their flat brandishing a gun and scaring the life out of them until they realised who it was, then they were not concerned anymore. This was not normal behaviour for a man of twenty, but it *was* for a boy of between nine and eleven, which was the behavioural age of Barry during this period of his life.

Barry's interest in guns and in all things military was born of our family's long association with the armed forces, just as in many other families in Britain. He'd have loved to be able to follow his dad's footsteps into the Army or the Royal Marines, he wanted to excel, but even the Territorial Army had to let him go because of his disabilities.

Pownall directed the jury to various folders during the trial. They contained a variety of exhibits: pictures and pertinent information provided for the jury, in binders, to take away with them when they eventually left to consider their verdict.

"Ladies and gentlemen of the jury, please open your photographic bundle and turn to the page I'm showing you here. That's right, the photograph of a coat."

The imposing prosecuting counsel held up a large, heavy file containing all the photographic evidence for this trial, some of which could certainly be described as sensitive and of a distressing nature.

"This is the defendant's coat, the one he says he may have been wearing on the day of the murder. The police seized this coat, along with other evidence, from the defendant's flat at 2b Crookham Road. When tested by forensic scientists, a single particle of firearms discharge residue was discovered in the inside pocket of the coat."

From my vantage point beside the dock, the courtroom was laid out before me in panorama. To the right of the room sat Mansfield and the defence team. Alongside were Pownall and the team for the prosecution. Sometimes there was an older woman there as well. I didn't realise until later that this was Alison Saunders of the Crown Prosecution Service. It seemed the magnitude of this trial merited her presence. She looked slightly out of place among the wigs and gowns, appearing a little uneasy in her attire of skirts and blouses. However, I was to learn in years to come that her benign look belied a sharp and uncompromising mind. The judge was elevated at the front of the court on the Bench, seated on a high-backed, red upholstered chair that could only be described as a throne, and the jury and witness stand were to my left.

Squinting, I tried to see what the jury had been directed to look at, but I was too far away to really make anything out. I was not entitled to view these pictures in case I decided to sell the distressing images to the media, though everyone seemed to have them but me, since they appeared in newspapers after the trial. The photo the jury was looking at was of a knee length, woollen Crombie-style coat, like the ones worn by businessmen in a British winter. The coat was obviously crumpled. It was on a tailor's dummy and had a white shirt under it with a red tie around the neck. Pownall was telling the jury that a single, microscopic particle of FDR had been found in the inside breast pocket of this garment.

"Likely, this was where the killer had put the gun to hide it from sight after the killing," he told them. The particle had been discovered by Robin Keeley of the Forensic Science Service, who was now the prosecution's expert witness.

The next photo in the series was of a gun and ammunition, said to be *similar* to that believed to have been used in the crime, since no guns were found in Barry's flat and the murder weapon has never been found. After this came the image of the microscopic particle, magnified thousands of times from its original size to make it visible. The fourth image was of the victim's hair.

Leading the jury through this sequence of images, Pownall spoke of the link between them all, the link to Barry George. The defendant's coat with the speck of residue on it, the gun, the cartridge case which would be covered in residue, and then the picture of the victim's head where he said the matching residue had been deposited at the time of the killing. This was proof that Barry George had killed Jill Dando.

What ensued after this was a week-long courtroom battle akin to a Dickensian drama, with billowing black gowns and woeful wigs and plentiful use of smoke and mirrors that led to one of the most infamous miscarriage of justice cases in recent British legal history. The saga surrounding Barry's coat is a tale of police incompetence and arrogance towards this man and to the legal process.

When the police seize an item it will be bagged and tagged in preparation for testing by the Forensic Science Service (FSS). Any evidence on or in the exhibit will be left undisturbed, and no innocent contamination should be possible. The bags are sealed, and the officer who seized the item will write their initials through the seal, indenting it, to make it impossible to tamper with the exhibit before inspection and analysis takes place. In the case of Regina v George, irregularities seem to have been the order of the day.

DC John Gallagher remained standing in the witness box after giving evidence to Pownall. He now awaited cross examination by Mansfield.

"Detective Constable Gallagher," Mansfield rested both hands on the lectern which held the bundle of papers he would refer to, or seem to refer to, while carrying out his cross examination of his witness, "would you please tell the court, in your own words, why you removed this defendant's coat, along with . . ." He looked down at his notes as though he had to check something in them, a theatrical gesture for the jury. "Oh yes, a black suit jacket and a red necktie. Tell the court why you took these sealed exhibits from the Exhibit Store, transported them in your car to a police photographic laboratory, opened the sealed bags and had the items photographed. Is this normal police procedure for exhibits?"

Leaning on the lectern as though he was about to do push-ups, Mansfield was now in full swing. His long straight silver hair glistening under a dull and tatty, beige, horse-hair wig, and his legal robe, threadbare and a shade of charcoal grey rather than black. He would never agree to replace it with a new one; this was his original robe from when he took silk in 1989.

The burly officer, DC Gallagher, looked briefly discomforted, his face a shade of embarrassed pink. I would not have been surprised if he had tucked a finger inside his collar and pulled on it, as if to loosen it. However, he held his composure as he cast a slightly arrogant glance around the court.

"We needed photographs of the coat and other items to show to identification witnesses," he replied, "to confirm whether this was the type of clothing they remembered seeing on the day of the murder." Head high now, he moved his gaze around the court as he delivered his explanation.

Mansfield looked up from his notes and held Gallagher's gaze firmly. "And these exhibits had already been tested by the Forensic Science Service, had they?" A defiant looked crossed Gallagher's face. "No, they were tested at a later date."

With an incredulous air, Mansfield began to outline what had happened to Barry's clothing before any testing had taken place.

"So, you removed the items from their sealed exhibit bags . . ." Mansfield, in a slow and deliberate tone, addressed the witness. " . . . placed your own white shirt from your wardrobe on the tailor's dummy, then put the tie and jacket on top."

I'd heard some of this before, but even I was stunned at the audacity of the police to rely on the integrity of these items as evidence in a murder case when they had compromised them so outrageously, flouting their own rules about the storage and safety of exhibits. According to the officer, the coat had been dropped onto the plastic carrying case which he had used to transport the sealed items, first to his car, then to his home to collect his shirt, and now to the studio.

Next, Barry's coat was thrown over a chair in the studio, allowing it to drape to the floor, while other photos were taken of the jacket, shirt and tie, according to DC Gallagher's testimony. The coat was then placed on the table where guns and ammunition had been photographed just days before. Later, it was draped over the tailor's dummy and various items of clothing before being folded, resealed, and passed to the FSS for testing. The woollen coat, which would readily shed fibres, would also readily retain fibres and debris from the environment.

When Mansfield asked expert witness, Robin Keeley of the FSS, whether he had *known* the coat had been removed from its packaging, before he tested it, Keeley answered, "No. I didn't know this until after I had reported the presence of the single particle of FDR to the police."

DC Gallagher was an officer who sometimes carried a weapon in the course of his duties, and no testing has ever been done to see how much FDR may be in our everyday environment. Technically, FDR is a compound of metals and does not break down over time or by washing or dry cleaning of garments. Residue may well be present in our day to day interactions with people and places. For example: a man pays for his shopping with notes from his pocket that has inadvertently been contaminated with FDR from his gun club, or the gun he uses on his farm. The next person given that note in their change, now transfers some of that contamination to *his* wallet . . . and so on. If environmental testing were to be carried out, say, on public transport seating, we may well find we *all* have some level of FDR contamination on or around us.

The only testing of the environment mentioned in court was of the FSS canteen, to check if their clean-room hygiene processes prevented contamination from spreading to the rest of the building via those who handled guns and firearms exhibits. The canteen routinely tested positive for FDR.

The debacle over whether the coat would or could have become contaminated at the studio went on for days, by which time this microscopic speck of FDR had become a mountain of evidence to the jury, thanks to the skilful tactics of the police and prosecution, which left the jury bamboozled.

"DC Gallagher," Mansfield ended his interrogation with a last loaded question, "since it was so important to take these pictures of the defendant's clothing that you would risk contaminating vital evidence in a murder case, can you tell us . . . how many witnesses you showed these photographs to? One . . . five . . . or maybe to all of them? How many witnesses saw these very important pictures?"

The one word answer spoke volumes.

"None."

Another piece of evidence, a microscopic blue-grey fibre, played a very minor role in the trial. The prosecution told the jury that it was discovered during forensic testing of Jill's raincoat and that it came from a pair of trousers owned by Barry. They made this claim even though this filament of fabric could not be fully tested because it was damaged by the testing process. Only one fibre was found.

The expert witness who was called by the prosecution testified that this was an uncommon dye and that it could be linked as a *match* to Barry's trousers. This was not the case. The trousers were from a well-known high street store and they would have sold many items made from the same fabric, such as suits and separates. This same fabric would probably have been used for garments sold into other retailers for their fashion lines, too. Ms Dando herself could have owned such a garment!

My indignation rose. *Are these people for real?* They are trying to sell this single, damaged fibre as an indisputable link to an atrocious murder. The police said Barry was wearing his woollen coat when he killed Jill. Barry's coat, with a texture like felt, would have shed its fibres readily at the scene. Why were there none of these on Ms Dando's coat if he had held her down at close quarters and shot her? This evidence was of no probative value, yet was being portrayed as a crucial find, linking this man, and this man only, to the killing of Jill Dando.

At the end of yet another strenuous day of listening to what was being said in court about Barry, and also the battle with the media as I entered and left the court followed by chatting with Mum to try to help her to cope with it all, I went upstairs to bed. This was the only place I could really get peace; there was no one demanding anything from me. Often, this would be my time to ring home to see how the family were doing. That particular night it was too late to ring, so I read a little and then settled down to sleep.

Suddenly, I was gripped by a burning tightness in my chest, making it difficult to breathe. *What is this, am I having a heart attack?*

Dear Lord, I prayed, *you know I am ready to come to you whenever you call, right now if you say so, but Lord, what about my poor mother? She will find me dead in bed in the morning, and she has already suffered so much. And Barry, Lord, he will think it was his fault. And what about my children, what will it do to them?*

Eventually the pain started to ease, and after a while I fell into a fitful sleep. On reflection next morning, I concluded it must have been the extreme stress that brought on that terrible experience. *I must take better care of myself,* I thought. This was a fearsome warning to watch my reaction to stress.

The end of the trial was drawing near and both sides presented their closing arguments. Predictably, Pownall went over all of the evidence he had imparted during the past seven weeks. When he had finished, I had to agree he sounded persuasive, and he really worried me. Then it was Mansfield's time. He disparaged much of what Pownall said and explained it away cogently. If Barry had been at HAFAD between 11am and 12, it was impossible for him to be the killer. Using that time frame, Barry could not have killed Jill at 11:30, walked off in the opposite direction to his home, changed his clothes and walked to the disability centre. It couldn't be done, therefore they had to acquit.

I felt a little more confident after that and felt sure the jury could not convict . . . not beyond reasonable doubt, and that *was* the legal standard. There were great gaping holes in the circumstantial evidence in this case against him.

Justice Gage read out his summing up to the jury. He directed the jury only to discuss the evidence when they were all together. They should tell the court usher if they had any questions and they would be brought back in to court to have those answered.

The closing arguments and summing up took days to complete. Then, on 26th June, the jury, now down to eleven members due to a bereavement for one of them, were told they would start their deliberations the next morning. Justice Gage instructed them to bring an overnight bag with them. They were to be sent to a hotel for the night if they hadn't reached a conclusion by the end of the day. Sequestering is rare in Britain and the jury members did not look pleased, but Justice Gage knew this case was much too sensitive to allow any outside influences to reach the jury.

We all hunkered down in the canteen of the Old Bailey to await the verdict. A few times we heard the call: All parties in Court One, please return to the courtroom. Each time our hearts leapt in trepidation, only to find the jury had a question. On Friday, Justice Gage took the unprecedented step of ordering the deliberations to continue on Saturday 30th. He also told the jury he would accept a majority verdict if they couldn't reach a unanimous one.

We had to be in court on that day, too, just in case the jury reached a decision, a day we would usually have used to visit Barry. Then, on Monday 2nd July, we were again summoned back to the courtroom. Another question? The commotion outside the doors indicated that this was different. Then we heard the whispers in the hall.

"It's a decision!"

Apprehensively, we filed back into court and took our places in front of the police and Jill Dando's family.

"Foreman of the jury, have you reached a verdict?"

"We have, my Lord."

10

Convicted

Guilty!
Just one little word, but it would change the course of so many lives. It was like a slap of ice water; a breath-taking shock. How was this possible?

There was an audible gasp from behind me where Jill Dando's friends and family sat alongside the police. I don't know if she was incredulous or relieved, but looking around the courtroom I was surprised at the looks of complete shock on the faces I saw. Pownall was looking to his team with his mouth hanging open. Apparently, he didn't expect to achieve a conviction. The gathering of journalists stood wide-eyed for a few seconds before suddenly recovering themselves and rushing from the courtroom, presumably to report the verdict to the waiting world.

At first, I couldn't catch sight of Barry because the guards from Belmarsh were standing in the way and blocking my view, but when they all turned to go down the steps to the cells in the bowels of the Old Bailey, I was able to make eye contact. Barry's sad brown eyes looked into mine, and his shoulder shrug seemed to say, *I don't understand, how did this happen?* In that one gesture, I read hurt, bewilderment, cynicism, fear, and defeat. I mouthed the words *"We'll fight",* but his expression remained disconsolate.

This was a life-shattering shock, and totally unexpected by many, especially since there was no evidence to connect him to the crime at all, just circumstantial bits and pieces that had been explained. If our justice system is predicated on 'beyond reasonable doubt', then there was nothing to base a guilty verdict on! Every piece of evidence submitted by the prosecution could be, and had been, countered by the defence team, though this was never reported in the press. I had waited in vain for Mansfield's arguments to appear in newspapers, or even on the TV news. It was a startling revelation to me when I realised that the media, who are only allowed into our courts in the public interest, just report the details from the prosecution side of a trial.

Looking back, I can see just how deeply I went into shock after Barry's conviction. I felt completely obliterated. My memories of this time are buried deep inside a pea-soup fog, and many have not resurfaced at all. There are holes where there should be a sequence of events in the aftermath of the jury's decision. I have no recollection of leaving the courtroom to go down to the waiting media outside in the street, yet I do recall writing out the family statement for Barry's solicitor to read for us in response to this devastating news.

Did I ring Mum to tell her the news? I can't be sure, maybe Mike did it. How did we get away from the media and home from the court? The answer is I just don't know the answers to these questions. Sometimes memories rise up tantalisingly out of the mists, only to dive back down, leaving part-formed images that I can't complete, bits and pieces that still haunt. This must be the mind's way of protecting itself from devastating overload, much like the response to the sudden death of a loved one. How much trauma and anguish can one mind take before it shatters under the strain?

We'd been left reeling. The shock of Barry's conviction was palpable. There were reporters knocking on Mum's door, ringing the bell, shouting through the letter box and dropping notes in. The house was under siege again, with everyone looking for a scoop. A pack of wolves were baying at the door!

I phoned the police to try to have them removed, but I was told there was nothing they could do: the media had the right to be there. It would seem we had been thrown to the dogs, fair game, just fodder for news stories. There was no law we could call on to protect us. Innocent of any crime or wrongdoing, we were imprisoned and could be sacrificed to a waiting public, just as Barry had been. What kind of justice was this? A woman had been murdered, her family devastated, and the British judicial system seemed happy to convict an innocent, mentally disabled man on circumstantial evidence and flawed police procedures. Surely this poor woman and her family deserved better? Convicting the wrong person could never be justice. If something happened to one of my family, a scapegoat would not appease me; I would want the *culprit* brought to justice, not just anybody put into prison. With Barry's arrest, the ripple effect encompassed his immediate family, then relatives, broader family, friends, neighbours and acquaintances. Now it had grown to include all of those affected by Ms Dando's death, too. Both families seeking justice, both receiving only a perversion, an injustice.

Where do we go to from here? I had no idea. I was numb and lost, adrift on an ocean. All I could think about was that there had to be a way to reverse this, but how could we achieve that? All the same feelings of bewilderment, fear and impotence that I'd felt at the time of Barry's arrest had risen to the surface again. The hand wringing, the agitated walk-about; hot and feverish one moment, shivering the next. We had three mobile phones between us and Mum's landline, and they all keep ringing. Sometimes it was friends and family, but frequently it was members of the press looking for an exclusive. The pack at the door was relentless.

Oh, Mum, I thought as I looked at the pitiful, shrunken woman before me. *You look as though you've taken a body blow.* Mum's health had been a concern for us all since the outset of this terrible experience. A slight woman at almost 5'1", she had always been deceptively strong . . . until now. The protracted illness she'd suffered leading up to the trial had left her severely weakened. All that kept her going was the belief that her son, an innocent man, could not be convicted of a crime he hadn't committed. Now that rug had been pulled from under her feet and she was floundering. She desperately wanted to go to the front door to give the hounds a piece of her mind, but I couldn't let her do that. That is exactly what they wanted. I could see the news headlines for the next day: *Dando killer's Mum shows true colours, treats reporters to torrent of abuse!*

The press had searched high and low for anything they could use to show Barry's family up, to portray us as more dysfunctional than The Simpsons. There was nothing to find, so I couldn't let her play into their hands at this stage. Of course, Mum was angry with me for stopping her from going outside, and I understood why, but I would take the brunt of her wrath a thousand times over rather than give media moguls more stories to get rich on.

Mike looked like a caged lion, prowling about in Mum's tiny two up, two down property. He was shaking his head from side to side and muttering swear words to himself about the legal system, the media and the police; all those who knew this was wrong, but let it go ahead just because there had to be a conviction to satisfy the public. He, too, wanted to speak with the vultures at the door, but this was not the time for an interview. We needed to think about what to do next. We had to know what we wanted to say to the newspapers and TV journalists. We needed space to think things through. Mike understood that need better than Mum, he just felt the need to try to fix this. Mum was too close; she was the woman who had given birth to this disabled man, and she loved him unconditionally.

Time became a blur and I don't know if we hid away in self-preservation for a day, or if it was two or three. It was obvious Mum would have to come home to Cork with me, I just had to work out how to get away from here without a media scrum following us.

We were still getting constant phone calls from TV channels and newspapers for interviews, but they were no longer camped outside the door, thanks to a caring neighbour. Mary had phoned us to see if she could do anything to help. She'd been really concerned for

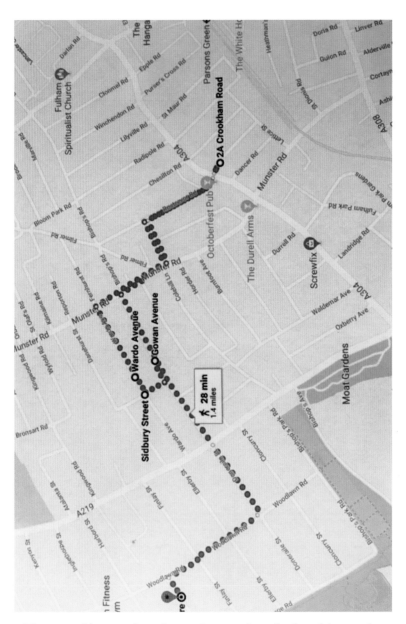

The impossible route the police say Barry took on the day of the murder.
This route takes 28 minutes and Barry still needed to change his clothes.

Credit: Google Maps

Mum and Dad's wedding day, 31st July 1954.

Mine and Pat's wedding day, 31st July 1982.
Credit: Barry's Photographic, Pembroke Street, Cork.

Mum and Barry.

The photo that caused the first trial to collapse.
The white forensic suit is visible around Barry's neck.

Taken on a prison visit. Shows Mike, Barry and mum.

Taken on the day of Barry's release, me addressing the
media with our family's statement.
Credit: Getty Images

Image of me taken by a journalist capturing my haunted look. What happened to our day of joy?
Credit: Getty Images

Addressing those assembled after the March from Runnymede, opposite the Houses of Parliament, 21st February 2015.
Credit: Paul Mockford.

Protesters with a Chris Grayling look-a-like head.

Placard waving protesters angry at the changes to legal aid and other cuts.
Many were solicitors and barristers.

Our protest against the new 'Not Innocent Enough' ruling in British justice, outside Westminster Hall, 21st February 2015.

Credit: Paul Mockford.

Some courageous women from JENGbA (Joint Enterprise Not Guilty by Association) who joined us to lend support.

Credit: Paul Mockford.

Barry with his placard held aloft.
Credit: Paul Mockford.

Myself and Barry smiling despite the chilly February day.
Credit: Paul Mockford.

Mum, and for all of us, when she'd heard Barry had been convicted. We, for our part, were embarrassed that there was a media frenzy outside of Mum's neighbours' homes. Mum's home was in a terrace, and we had already witnessed people trying to access their own homes being blocked by reporters. My phoning the police to have the legion removed had had no effect.

When this concerned neighbour rang us, I apologised to her for the melee outside her home and explained that I been told by the police that they were within their rights to be there. Her lovely soft Irish burr was gentle and full of compassion . . . until she heard this. Now, gone was the soft voice. Her outraged response reverberated across the phone line and we all smiled for the first time.

"What? Those filthy rotten b*****ds, well they'll move them for me!" With that, she hung up.

Ten minutes later, she rang back. "I told those so-and-sos to get those cameras and journalists out of here. My children can't go outside to play, and none of us want them annoying us when we try leave our homes!"

Within minutes, the media encampment had dispersed and an uneasy peace descended on our battle-scarred home.

During this period of post-conviction turmoil, a diversity of opinions emerged about what should be done. Mike and I were all for mounting a campaign to fight on, and Mike took many a knock because he wouldn't stop talking about taking this forward. My cousins were all for us continuing our fight to have Barry released because they had never considered that he could have been guilty in the first place. We had all grown up together and it was well accepted that Barry had some serious issues because of his disabilities, but he was not a criminal genius, nor was he a murderer.

There were other family members who were also for us continuing, they just wanted to stay well out of the media glare, which was completely understandable. Then, there were those within our circle who believed he was guilty: he must have been, because the courts said so. I have noticed in life that there are people who delight to see the downfall of another's family because then their family does not look so dysfunctional. Many of us watch TV programmes about out-of-control hoarders with glee, and this is a prime example of this phenomenon. Anybody's home looks good after seeing that level of mess and mayhem.

Still, others believed that all was lost, that there was no way anyone could fight against a machine the size of the Great British Justice System, so we should just accept the conviction and get on with our own lives.

"It's done now, there's nothing anyone can do to change it. You'll just have to visit him in the prison until he's released, he'll be out in about eight years." This was the pragmatic stance of one family member. "You can't fight the whole justice system."

Sitting slumped forward in the armchair, my shoulders hunched and my soul depleted, I looked from one to the other and thought, *Yes, they're right, this is a battle we can never win. Maybe it is time to give it all up.* Then, from somewhere deep in the pit of my being, a new thought struggled to be born. It was hot and insistent, carried aloft as if it were being pushed upwards on a tide of lava . . .

We may not be able to fight this colossus . . . *but God can.*

11

Campaign Launch

That first night after the conviction, I don't know how we eventually decided it was time to go to bed. Who wanted to *sleep*? Sleep is a normal function; nothing about our lives now was normal. We were the walking wounded.

I don't recall going up to bed, but I did sleep – complete mental and physical exhaustion must have seen to that. We must have gotten up the next day, too, though I don't remember that either. At some stage there was a phone call on my mobile from Paddy Hill. He wanted to know if I would agree to be interviewed by Trevor McDonald for his news show on ITN. It seems that having failed to reach me themselves, they had gotten hold of Paddy.

It was the last thing I wanted to do, expose us all to the media glare again, but Paddy had a long chat with me, explaining that at some stage I would have to speak with someone. We would never get any peace until I did. It was better to speak with someone well respected like Trevor, and it would be a chance to start fighting back, to let everyone know that we did not accept this conviction and would be seeking an appeal.

In a daze, I agreed, and it was set up that myself and Mum would be picked up and brought to a top London hotel for this interview. We were to be fully packed for travelling back to Cork because, although there would not be a fee for this interview, the programme makers would fund our fares home. If a fee *had* been available, I would not have accepted it anyway. It would have felt like blood money.

Because everything of mine would be packed for the journey back to Ireland, I asked if there would be someone to tidy my hair and do my makeup at the hotel, since this was what was available when I had done other TV interviews before the conviction. This wasn't vanity, it was because the lighting used during filming is very intense, and programme makers know that special makeup is required just to appear normal. I was assured by TV representatives that I could pack everything into my case as there would certainly be a makeup person there.

We arrived at the hotel in central London at about 6am, tired and dishevelled, having left home at close to 5am. We had a quick coffee, and breakfast was offered, but I couldn't eat. I was much too nervous. When the programme people arrived, I looked around for the familiar and reassuring face of Trevor McDonald, but he was nowhere to be seen. Then we were told he would not be doing the interview after all; it was to be carried out by a man named Martin Bashir. This name meant nothing to me because I lived in Ireland and rarely watched British TV. We were assured that he was a well-respected interviewer, so I reluctantly agreed to sit and talk with him about doing this programme. I had been ready to walk out and make my own way back to Cork, but was persuaded that this was not necessary: Mr Bashir would take good care of us, and Trevor had sent him as his best man for the job.

We sat in the plush hotel lobby for a while and talked, discussing what would be coming up in this interview, the areas to be explored. Obviously, some topics would be uncomfortable to talk about, but there was nothing too daunting here. I decided to go ahead and be interviewed by this unknown man. Mr Bashir told me with pride that he had done the interview with Princess Diana, but I didn't know much about that, either.

I said silent prayers that God would put his hand of protection over me, help me to speak clearly and put our case for Barry's innocence across concisely. We were already living in the middle of a maelstrom and I didn't need more confusion, or to say something that would be taken out of context. The British public needed to know that this was not over, that we were going to fight for Barry and for justice.

The hotel was one of those wonderfully laid out structures in glass and steel, with indoor gardens at the centre, vaulted ceilings, potted palms and a flowing waterfall splashing down into a large ornamental pool. I would have loved to walk around and enjoy the interior design, since this was of great interest to me, but this was not the time. Serious business was at hand; I had to pass all of this by and get into the waiting elevator with Mum, Paddy Hill and Mr Bashir. There were three young women there, too, from the studio, along with a couple of guys. It was quite a squash. I presumed one of these women was a make-up person. I was really going to need her skills today. I was a wreck! I had deep black eyes, with red rims from crying. My face was pale and blotchy and my hair, though clean, was tatty with neglect.

Alighting the elevator at some anonymous floor, we walked the corridor to an equally anonymous door, and entered the room. As I stepped over the threshold, I looked about me and suddenly anger rose up through my body like bile. I tried to stay calm and give the benefit of the doubt to the TV personnel; this was probably not a set up, but a mistake that could be rectified.

"Am I sitting in the wing-backed chair?" I asked, pointing to a high-backed chair placed on a floor that was covered in what looked like various coloured snakes criss-crossing the room, anchored down to the carpet with black tape. There were steel poles and huge white umbrellas set up around the room, along with a sound boom covered in one of those big fluffy sheaths, and a fixed camera. The only other seating in the room was a small, two-person couch in red leather, just big enough for a couple of kids. It was low slung and squashy-looking.

Mr Bashir looked at me and smiled. "No, that's mine. I'm afraid the room has already been set up for filming now, you and your Mum should be fine there," he said, pointing to the kiddie couch.

The anger I had been holding down started to surface again.

"What? Do you really think we're going to sit there? Firstly, my mother is not part of this interview, and secondly, I am not going to sit in that low-slung seat. It's an insult. You know if I sit there I will be scrunched up, I'll look like the Michelin Man!" This was a tactic of the media's I had come across before. "Please get me a chair like yours so we can be equals here."

Goodness, my mind whispered. *That was brave of you Michelle, where did that courage come from?*

Mr Bashir's response was that this was not possible, but that the two studio guys would be able to lift the seating level. "They'll boost the couch with extra cushions and it won't be noticeable in the finished film," he assured me, pleading with me to continue.

This interview was not for me, it was for Barry, who was powerless to do anything in his own defence. I had to compromise for his sake, so I agreed that if this glitch with the seating could be rectified then I would continue. Then I asked to meet the make-up person, presuming she was in the little anteroom, where Mum was sitting in rather a discomforted state due my lack of subservience.

"We don't have a make-up person here, but you look fine," was the comment from my esteemed interviewer.

"You cannot be serious!"

What more could go wrong? *Lord, you have to help me here. This is a comedy of errors, except it's not in the least bit funny. I just don't know what to do. I can't go on camera looking like this, straight from bed, dishevelled, as though I've been pulled through a bush backwards.*

What do I do, Lord?

This was a serious interview, it was the announcement of our determination to start a campaign, to fight back. It was not a brief look into the lives of two pitiable women, broken and defeated.

Mum was speaking from the other room. "It's alright. Just do it, so we can go." She looked extremely uncomfortable sitting in the chair in the small room, but it was my assertiveness that was causing her the discomfort, not the seat.

One of the three young women intervened, realising that I was at my wits' end and about to depart. "Why don't we see if we can cobble together some make-up from all of our handbags? We're bound to find something that works."

We tipped everything out of the handbags and onto the bed. Coins and tampons, keys, and whatever cosmetics they carried with them tumbled out onto the old-fashioned candlewick bedspread. Using all my skills and some inventive measures, I managed to hide the shadows around my eyes and made myself look presentable for the camera. Then, using the hotel's fixed-to-the-wall hairdryer and a hastily procured hairbrush, we tamed the hedgehog that was my hair. I was ready. It was a great help to my spirit, too, to be able to have a few giggles with the girls in the bathroom; it lightened the mood.

Composing myself again, I entered the room where the crew were waiting and tested the altered seating, suggesting some more boosting when my midsection disappeared beneath my bust, making me look like the Pillsbury Doughboy. The guys bustled around again and eventually the seat was upright enough to not make me look or feel at a disadvantage. Surely it would have been easier to ring hotel reception and ask for the use of another wing backed chair?

We were both miked up. The interview was underway. Mr Bashir introduced me to the ITN viewers, explaining who I was and why I was being interviewed. We chatted comfortably for a while, with me parrying questions, silently praying that God would protect me from any harm.

Then it came . . . out of the blue, the question we had not discussed. "Your father was a violent man, wasn't he?"

I was completely thrown. Where had this come from? Not wishing the public to think that I refused to answer a question, I made a blithe remark about different times and different thoughts on disciplining children. I thought this would suffice, but I began to think my interviewer must have his own agenda here when he suggested again, "Yes, but he was very violent to you and Barry, wasn't he?"

Where could he possibly be going with this? *Lord, please help me to understand why he's posed this question.*

A blinding light-bulb moment filled my brain and the agenda became clear. I know I am not the sharpest tool in the box, and sometimes it can take a while for me to cop on to what's happening, but now I believed I knew where this was leading. At Barry's conviction, the Judge had uttered these words during his summing up: "We may never know why you did this . . ." That was because the prosecution could find no motive for Barry to have carried out this terrible crime. Maybe Mr Bashir thought *he* could be the one to supply a reason to the waiting world. He would solve the riddle!

Was he really trying to imply it was my father's fault?

Outrageous! As if our family was not suffering enough already, now it seemed someone wanted to make my Dad responsible for Jill Dando's terrible murder! *God, God, you have to help me stop this, what can I do? I can't let this man do this. Haven't we been victimised enough, must I now stand up to protect my father, too?*

Reaching up to the microphone clip attached to the inside of my blouse, I unclipped it and got up to leave the interview, much to Mr Bashir's complete astonishment. Whatever response he was expecting, this was clearly not it.

"No, no come back," he cried. "We can sort this out." He was apparently terrified that I would leave.

"I will not continue down this road with you. You will not put the blame for Jill's death on my father. He has nothing to do with any of this. How could he, *since Barry didn't kill her?* There is no connection between Jill and my father. This is outrageous, and if you want to continue this interview, this stops now!"

Where did I get the audacity to walk away like that? I am not usually that brave. My poor mother was in the other room listening to this and I knew she'd be cringing now. As I looked back at Mr Bashir, I caught sight of the film crew and of the girls peeking out from the other room. They were clearly enjoying this scene; they were all, rather unsuccessfully, trying to hide their grins.

I agreed to continue with the assurance that this topic was off-limits. The parrying began anew and, low and behold, he asked the same question. To do this twice was bad enough, but three times, to my mind, proved there was an agenda here.

This time, I didn't honour it with an answer. Stripping off the microphone, I again headed for the anteroom. "Come on Mum, it's time to go."

"Mr Bashir," I said with all the contempt I could muster, "you can go back to your boss and tell him I refused to continue with this interview."

He came rushing after me, begging me to continue, telling me what a wonderful opportunity I would miss. It was the chance to tell the world about the case, Barry's innocence, and our campaign. I was surprised to see beads of sweat on his face. He again managed to get me to agree to continue, and this time the interview was brought to its completion without incident.

Mr Bashir held out his hand to shake mine as I collected Mum and prepared to depart. Shaking his hand, I again noted the beads of sweat on his face. *He'll edit that out before it goes on air*, I thought.

"Thank you for the interview, Michelle," he said, pumping my hand. "And remind me never to have an argument with *you!*" was his parting quip.

When the programme aired a few days later, the beads of sweat were still clearly visible. In contrast, I appeared calm, relaxed and powdered. They really should have had a make-up person.

Dear Lord, thank you for your protection.

The thought of returning home to Cork after Barry's conviction filled me with mixed feelings. Yes, I wanted to be home with my family, my church family and my old life, but I had to wonder about how we would be treated now that Barry had been found guilty. I had dreamt of our triumphant homecoming, but now I wondered if people would think we should wear sack-cloth and ashes and hang our heads in shame. Would we be ostracised? Would there be some who would shout abuse at us in the street?

Paddy Hill decided to come to Cork with us, and I was so grateful. As an Irish exoneree of the British justice system, he was treated like a returning hero; everybody wanted to stop and talk with him. If it had been now, he would have been asked for 'selfies' everywhere we went. His presence gave our case credibility in the eyes of the people we met. We were treated like returning combatants.

Mum stayed with us in Cork for a couple of weeks to build up her strength, but she would stay no longer. "My Barry is in that awful place with no one to visit him. I must go back," she insisted.

The media's phone calls and text messages didn't stop after I arrived home, I just chose to ignore them as I regrouped, ready for whatever would come next.

We still lived in this real world of children, school, work and the mundane day to day stuff of life. My time at college had ended some time ago and I was working at Irish Guide Dogs for the Blind, on Model Farm Road, just a fifteen minute walk from home. It was hard facing workmates day to day, some of whom were not sympathetic to our family, preferring to believe the salacious stories in the press rather than the truth. Painful as that was, I was well aware that there would always be people like that in the world, so I thanked God for those who were supportive, held my head up and got on with living.

About three weeks after the conviction, the house phone rang just as I was leaving to go to work.

"Hello, Mrs Diskin?"

Oh, no, I thought to myself. *Time to turn off autopilot and switch to wary mode.*

"Mrs Diskin, my name is Linda, and I'm a researcher on RTÉ's Gerry Ryan Show on FM radio 2. Gerry would really like to interview you about the recent conviction of your brother, Barry George, for the murder of Jill Dando." She went on to say that she knew I was not giving interviews at the moment, but maybe I'd like to tell the nation what we were intending to do. "Are you accepting this conviction or will you appeal?"

Accepting? I could feel my hackles rise.

"No, we do not accept this!" I almost growled at the poor girl.

"Then this is a chance to come on Gerry's show and tell the nation," she encouraged.

The Gerry Ryan Show was the one I'd been waiting to listen to on that fateful day when I heard the news of Barry's arrest.

Cautious of being interviewed via the phone, I insisted on being in the studio with Gerry. I wanted to see his face and read his expressions. RTÉ brought me to Dublin along with my eldest daughter, Carine, so we could have some mother/daughter time. I waited in the studio till it was my time to go on air. Gerry's show was two hours long, and I had been scheduled into the second 20 minute slot. It was planned that we would discuss the case on air, and then have a brief phone-in for the listeners.

The interview went down so well with the listeners that Gerry let me know the third 20 minute slot story had been postponed because there was so much interest in Barry's case. He asked if I would be willing to stay on air. Our interview went on for the remainder of the airtime.

Afterwards, Gerry thanked me profusely and said how much he admired what I was doing, even though he wasn't sure if Barry was innocent or guilty. He remarked that the listeners had taken me to their hearts, saying that if they were in trouble, they would want me on their side.

"Can I give you a little advice, Michelle? Well, I'm going to anyway," he said, grinning at me. Then his face went grave again. "Do *not* make this your life's work, please. I have seen people who have done this and they become shadows of themselves. I'd hate to see that happen to you."

What a kind and thoughtful man. I promised Gerry I had no intention of letting that happen, but I was truly touched by his words. I was terribly upset when I heard the tragic news of his death in April 2010; I had so hoped to meet him again.

The Gerry Ryan Show wasn't the only interview I agreed to do during this aftermath period. There were two documentaries produced for Channel 4 television, both of which discredited the evidence that had been used to convict Barry. I took part in the first of these, which was made shortly after Barry's conviction and when I was still terrified of the media and the power it could wield. Add to that Barry's paranoia, and his angry protests that I should not speak to anyone, TV or otherwise, it's understandable that I had to be persuaded over and over that this was in Barry's interest and not against him before I would co-operate.

The second was made by the same producer, James Cohen and his team, to coincide with Barry's second appeal in 2007. BBC's Panorama with Raphael Rowe also made a documentary at this time, managing to get admonished by the judiciary for their timing; it aired before the court sitting! These were all very important documentary works clearly pointing to a miscarriage of justice in Barry's case.

After a while, life became less frenetic and I took advantage of the calm before the storm to take up my old life again, my Irish life. It was still necessary for me to travel to the UK, though. I needed to visit Mum and Barry, and sometimes meet with journalists and TV programme makers. The BBC and Sky News channels would contact us whenever a new story broke, or a supposed exposé was revealed by salacious newspaper reporting. I can vividly remember the feeling of dread when the News of the World ran a story alleging Barry had confessed and that they had an audio tape, smuggled out of the prison, to prove it! This tape was put up on a phone-in for the public to listen to even before the police had studied it. Of course we knew he was not guilty, so what did this mean?

The following week the Daily Mail printed the same story. Their headline: 'Prison Cell Confession' by killer of Jill Dando. None of these articles were true, the 'recording' was indistinct and obviously spliced together, but the public were led to believe he had confessed. They were never told that the tape had been formally discredited, or that many prisoners gave statements to say that they knew this was staged by another prisoner for money, a dangerous criminal they would not go up against. Also, no one could tell us how audio tapes could be smuggled *out* of a prison, when we couldn't smuggle in a paper tissue!

12

Appeals and the CCRC

After the first shock of the conviction had receded, it was time to get back to work. Barry was innocent and we could not let this injustice continue. Having laid the groundwork with the media interviews, we needed to back that up with some legal activity.

I visited Barry in Whitemoor Prison, a Category A men's facility in Cambridgeshire. This was where he had been sent after conviction, because there was no need to have him in London if he wasn't attending court. Hazel Keirle of MOJO was working on all the evidence in the case to pull out the pertinent areas for appeal, such as the ID evidence, the FDR and Barry's visit to HAFAD. We had had many a late night discussion on the phone because I was at home in Cork. I will always be grateful to her for this. I was certainly not equipped to write a legal submission to the Criminal Cases Review Commission (CCRC) myself.

Barry's first appeal in 2002 had been rejected. We'd been both shocked and excited to get an appeals hearing just six months after conviction. This seemed like good fortune, as though the justice system had realised there'd been an error and were anxious to correct it. I was wrong. They hadn't accepted any of the arguments put forward by Mansfield and the defence team on ID evidence, scientific evidence, or the role of the judge at trial. Mansfield had a statement from Reverend John Hale, Barry's pastor at the Baptist church he attended in Fulham, given after conviction, stating he had been visiting Barry's apartment on the 18th May 2000, and had encountered three armed officers, one with a rifle type firearm and two with handguns. Reverend Hale had also told me this himself when I attended Sunday service whilst in the UK. In a letter from Reverend Hale to Marilyn Etienne, dated 16th May 2002, he states that she considered it would be 'unfruitful to pursue this matter further with me'. He ends with 'I consider I have discharged my duty to truth and justice in this matter'. He did not appear in court, to give evidence, he wasn't called. The police said Reverend Hale is a nice person, but that he was mistaken.

The three high court judges took two hours to read out their reasons for turning down the appeal. That day in court was hugely traumatic for us all. Mum had come to court. She was finally feeling stronger and more able to cope, and she wanted to be there when they released her son so that she could take him home.

As we sat waiting for the judgement, it was clear that everyone there, legals, media and Barry, already knew the outcome. Everyone, that is, except us! The verdict had been given out to journalists and legals, but we were not entitled to have access to that document. If it hadn't been for a MOJO representative showing us the refusal, we would have sat there for two hours still thinking Barry was coming home.

That was bad enough, but worse was to come. Between the time of hearing the appeal some months earlier and the reading out of the verdict, Barry's plastic little pellet-shooting replica gun, a children's toy, had become a Kalashnikov rifle in the minds of the Judges! This information was duly read out to the court and although everyone there knew this was untrue, nobody corrected them, so it was reported in all the papers.

In September of 2002, on a visit to Barry, I excitedly informed him of our next move.

"Barry, we're going to put in a submission to the CCRC on your behalf. We're exploring all avenues to get you cleared and released." I thought Barry would be overjoyed that we were working so hard on his behalf but, inexplicably, he was spitting feathers!

"I don't want you or MOJO to do that. My solicitor is going to get me out. She's going to the House of Lords. There's no evidence against me, I'll be out by Christmas," he informed me. "Don't you and MOJO go making things worse for me. Loads of guys in here said to keep away from MOJO. My solicitor is my only hope."

He looked near apoplectic, but this was not unusual. Barry always knew 'the best way' for things to be done, and Mum, Mike and I had fallen foul of his snappy remarks on many a visit. Indeed, both myself and Mike had threatened to leave him to it during visits where we were given orders on what we could and could not do. I remember saying, "Okay, Barry, if you continue to be so nasty, I'm leaving. My children are at home in Cork without me, I'm here trying to help you. I will not stay to battle against you. Do as you please!"

I would walk to the door of the visits room. Usually Mum would try to intercede. Poor Mum, there was a limited amount of time given to visit him and she didn't want it wasted. Of course, I didn't want that either. My time was precious, too, time taken from my own family's needs to be there. If Barry could spit feathers, well, so could I. Of course, it did concern me that he was being swayed by people who obviously were not on his side: any wrongly convicted prisoner would give their eye-teeth to be supported by MOJO. I decided to submit the document to the CCRC despite Barry's protestations.

Hazel Keirle and I went to Birmingham to the headquarters of the CCRC on 5th November 2002 to hand in the submission. Hazel had compiled it all on my behalf. This was not how MOJO usually worked. It should be the defendant who requests MOJO to work on their case, because not every defendant can trust their family. However, it was understood that this was an exceptional circumstance because of Barry's vulnerability, and therefore they would work with me to help him.

Not everyone in the family was pleased I had taken this upon myself, but these were uncharted waters and I knew we might need the CCRC if Barry lost at the House of Lords. The CCRC could refer his case back to the Court of Appeal. Of course, this meant yet another trip away from my family. I found these absences painful and the loneliness crippling. However, this was crucial, and we knew Barry's solicitors would be able to add to these submissions if they needed to.

On the 16th December 2002, we received the news that the House of Lords had turned down Barry's appeal and refused permission for him to mount any further challenges. So much for relying on his solicitor getting him out by Christmas. Barry was devastated. He had pinned his hopes on this and on his solicitor, believing he'd be coming home.

Appealing against conviction is a long, drawn-out and complicated process, like navigating through a fog for the uninitiated. When Barry's legal team had appealed, they'd had to seek leave to appeal within twenty-eight days after the conviction. Lower courts have a different time scale. The defence must have new evidence, something that had not been available at the time of the trial. This is almost an impossibility. Surely if there had been more evidence of innocence, it would be have been produced at trial? Where can a defendant get new evidence while they are incarcerated? There's no funding for a defendant to carry out any investigations because they are innocent until proven guilty. It is the prosecution who get the funding. Also, if the evidence had been available to the police, such as mobile phone photos or social media pages, even though it was not disclosed, would it be considered 'new'?

The problem with the Court of Appeal is they are only looking to see if the conviction is safe. Was the law as it stood used correctly? They do not look at guilt or innocence. The factually innocent can, and do, remain in prison because their conviction is deemed to be safe to the letter of the law. These three judges upheld Barry's conviction, the appeal was turned down, and Barry stayed in prison.

It was the same with the appeal to the House of Lords. Innocence was not the criteria for them, either, it was again the safety of the conviction. The refusal by the House of Lords for permission to mount any further challenges meant Barry could not apply to the

Court of Appeal again . . . basically, he could not waste their valuable time. Hazel Keirle had anticipated this, and was concerned at the delay Barry might face, which was why she wanted to get a submission into the CCRC as soon as possible.

The Criminal Cases Review Commission was established on 1st April 1997 in the wake of the terrible injustices toward mainly Irish people in the 1970s. These people could not get justice at that time, partly because of the political situation in Britain. They spent many painful years in prison claiming innocence. It was recognised that there was a need for an independent body to review cases like theirs, cases where it was likely the appellants were factually innocent.

Thank goodness that the CCRC exists today. When a defendant has exhausted the appeals process, this is the only way to get a case looked at again. We put all of the disputed evidence into Barry's submission, along with what we deemed to be new evidence. We advised others to give statements to them as well. They would be his saviour . . . except they wouldn't. They were hog-tied.

The CCRC were brought into existence to review cases for the wrongly convicted where there is a strong possibility that a factually innocent person is in jail. They are purported to be independent of the court system, even though they are funded by the government. A big problem is that they also have to review cases where a criminal wants to appeal against the length of a sentence, or cases such as that of a dog that was due for destruction under the Dangerous Dogs Act 1991. Dealing with such cases uses up vital resources, both financial and in man-hours. This leaves a paucity of both when cases of wrongful conviction come in. They end up in the background, waiting for the time and money necessary to deal with them. Also, the CCRC does not investigate cases to ascertain guilt or innocence. I had thought that was their primary function, but Barry waited seven years to gain his freedom.

As for the independence of the CCRC, they act more like a filtering service for the Court of Appeal. The test of whether a case should be referred back to the Court of Appeal is the 'real possibility' test, meaning, is there a real possibility the court will overturn the conviction? To my mind, this is the same as making the decision for them. It is the factually innocent who suffer, and the country foots the bill to keep innocent people locked up. Where are the guilty? Walking free in our neighbourhoods.

13

The Intervening Years

The intervening years between Barry's conviction and eventual release seemed interminable, but actually spanned seven years. Seven long years lived in a kind of limbo where we couldn't get on with our normal lives, nor do much to secure Barry's release. With no clear idea of how to run a campaign, our battle was less a structured attack, and more a determination not to tolerate this injustice. It was a *standing up* to say; no, this isn't right and we do not accept it.

As a family, we found ourselves living a stilted life, a life overshadowed by this wrongful conviction, this huge, far-reaching injustice. Waking each morning, I felt the cold fingers of doom clutched around my heart; we were no freer than Barry was. Thank God for the children. Life can't be lived in stasis when there are children to be nurtured, meals to be prepared, school runs to be organised, and bedtime prayers to be said. Therefore, we had to find a way to keep going which would not damage them, even though they could not be entirely unaffected by the disaster in their midst.

Pat and I both knew that my absences were very painful for the children as I kept up my regular visits to England to visit Barry and to check up on Mum's health. The only way I could think to alleviate their distress was to schedule individual and meaningful time with each of them. I knew that paying for extra airfares would be difficult but, as I was now back earning, I planned to take them one at a time to visit their Nana in London.

Pat agreed with me, and I managed to take one trip over to London with each child. It was so hard to organise and more so to fund. I made a conscious decision not to take them to see Barry even though they wanted to go. I just didn't want them to experience the ordeal of prison security. Having said that, I do think it helped them to see what it was that I did while I was away.

Mum visited with us far more often, though, which helped a lot. I also planned special time with each of them while I was at home in Ireland. They had a morning out with me on their own once a month, their quality time, when they didn't need to clamour for my attention. We'd go out to breakfast, go on a shopping trip, or maybe visit a relative in Limerick.

Our lives had changed. What had been normality was gone forever. Now we had to forge a new life, one that incorporated journalists, fake news and tapped phones again.

The press had backed off a bit, now that I was now conducting the occasional interview and outlining our campaign. I'd received many phone calls and letters from various people, often looking to offer encouraging words or to pass on information. Then one morning, when I was alone in the house, having taken the children to school, I answered a rather worrying phone call.

"Is that Barry George's sister?"

"Yes, it is . . . who's calling, please?"

"I'm not going to tell you my real name for security reasons, but you'll probably remember a Mr V being talked about in the Dando case. That's me. The police interviewed me about the murder right at the beginning. I thought they were going to pin it on me, so I lied about where I was at the time. Then they pinned it on your brother. I'm worried again now, because of him going to the CCRC . . . Maybe they'll come after me again, and I don't want that."

The man's tone was slightly threatening, but I continued to listen. At the end, I realised he was actually just scared. He thought we'd point the finger at him to free Barry. He then said he had more information about that day, but he wouldn't go to the police with it.

"Mr V," I spoke slowly and calmly, hoping to disarm his fears, "be assured, we are not interested in another scapegoat, and we are not investigating Jill Dando's murder, either. We're not equipped to do that. It's a police job. If you really feel you have information that might help Barry, and you don't trust the police, you will need to speak with the CCRC. They'll look at it."

My biggest concern here was that I didn't truly know the identity of the caller. He might have been a journalist seeking fodder for a story, or he might have been a crackpot, and I didn't want to engage with someone dangerous. I had a family to protect, and I would not sacrifice their safety. I made it a policy not to be the go-between for the CCRC. If there was information, it needed to be given to them in a statement.

My scariest moment came when I opened my front door one day to find a diminutive young man with a broad Scottish accent standing there. He wanted to come in and talk to me, but there was no way that was happening! Although it seemed bad mannered, we stood at the door, me with my foot braced around the jam, as if that was capable of repelling invaders.

He said his life was in danger from criminal gangs in Scotland, but he had information about Jill Dando's death, and that the gun that killed her had been used in another crime. Real or imagined, this young man was clearly terrified. He kept looking over his shoulder to make sure no one had followed him. He spoke of gangs and drugs, hitmen and guns and killings, and of the contract he believed had been taken out on Jill Dando's life because of her work on Crimewatch.

The urge to put my hands over my ears, like a child does, and shout 'La, La, La' at the top of my voice was so strong. I didn't want to hear this! This was not the safe, rather lacklustre world we inhabited; this was totally alien. It was clear that the line between our world and the nightmare world that this young man dwelt in was becoming blurred, but I could not allow his world to bleed into ours.

When Pat came home from work, I told him about Timmy, and he was visibly shaken. Timmy came back twice more over the next two days, but we never felt safe and didn't allow him into our home. We didn't see him again after that, but I always hoped he had escaped the assassination he so clearly feared.

From day one, when I first found out about Barry's arrest, fear became a constant companion. Fear of the unknown. Fear of the influence held by the media. Fear for Barry in prison. He was under a repressive regime and he was so vulnerable. Was his health being adequately monitored, was he safe from other, more violent inmates? I thought of this fear as the tentacles of terror. Those insidious arms infiltrated every area of my life, worming their way into the subconscious to eat away at my confidence, at my very foundations.

Worse still was the effect on my own sense of security, fear for personal safety. Mike voiced his fears for his safety to me many times. Publicly fighting for Barry left him feeling vulnerable and exposed. He found himself looking over his shoulder . . . was there a danger? Would he be stopped at the ferry port, and if he was, how would anyone know what had happened to him? Then, on March 4th 2001, a bomb went off outside the BBC headquarters in White City, one stop along the Underground from Mum's home.

BBC News:

Police say a bomb which exploded outside the BBC's main news centre in London was the work of an Irish dissident group.

Alan Fry, head of Scotland Yard's Anti-Terrorist Branch, said the blast went off as bomb squad officers were trying to carry out a controlled explosion of the suspicious vehicle at 0030GMT on Sunday.

It was "clearly a big device", which contained high explosives.

He said police had received a coded warning shortly beforehand, prompting them and the BBC to evacuate the premises. One London Underground worker suffered deep cuts to his eye from flying glass.

Fry said the explosion was an escalation of the Real IRA's terror campaign on mainland Britain.

It is believed to be the first such attack on the BBC.

Mike was so relieved that he had already left London and was en route to the ferry port when the blast occurred, though he continued to feel concerned. The horrors for the Irish after the Birmingham and Guildford pub bombings were still vividly painful. When Mum and I went to see Barry in Belmarsh after that incident, he also was quite distressed. He said he was glad he was locked up because otherwise they'd have picked him up for this, too, because he used to work at the BBC when he was fifteen. Barry really believed that. That, of course, was Barry's default position when anything happened. It only needed a tenuous link and his fears surfaced. That was what happened to him after he heard about Jill's awful death.

I hadn't realised just how scared Mum was, either, until one day she said to me, "Don't go telling people I live on my own, they might try to break into my place, you hear such awful stories." Of course, she knew of other families fighting injustice who had been viciously attacked because they stood up for their loved one. No wonder she was fearful for her safety, Jill Dando was a national treasure and her son was accused of her murder.

Various friends and family voiced their fears for me, as well.

"Michelle, you must be very careful. You're speaking out against the system, you might also get arrested on trumped up charges. And don't forget about the criminal fraternity – you're going up against some very scary people."

Their apprehensions were perfectly rational in the light of what had happened to Barry. This whole situation was larger than anything any of us had ever encountered. I thought of the horror of being wrongfully sent to prison, of my children's terror if I was incarcerated in a British jail. I also thought about the hideous fate of Jill Dando.

These were dangerous thoughts, thoughts that had the power to paralyse me into inaction. It would have been so easy to cower under such terrors, to run away. Instead, I turned to God, put my faith in him and took his words to my heart and made them mine. Verses such as Romans 8:31 –

> *"What, then, shall I say in response to these things? If God is for me, who can be against me?"*

Philippians 4:13 has become the maxim for my life:

> *"I can do all things through Christ who strengthens me."*

Inexorably, life moved on. Then one day I received a letter, then a follow up phone call, from a tentative young man working at University College Cork. His name was Gerard McCarthy and he had heard of Barry's case. He wondered if I would be willing to come and speak with some of his students who were taking Legal Studies.

"It's a small group, Michelle, and they're a friendly bunch," he quipped. "They've expressed a strong interest in understanding your brother's case better. Would you come and give them some more information, maybe explain the evidence and talk about his disabilities?"

It took a lot of persuading on his part, but eventually I agreed. This was the start of a new venture for me. It always astonished me that highly educated people would be interested in anything I had to say about the legal system, and it still does, but I see it as a responsibility to show the other side of the coin for students of law: miscarriage of justice and its effects.

After that I was asked by MOJO to speak at some of their meetings, where I've been privileged to meet some very august people in human rights. I've also spoken for other miscarriage of justice campaign groups, including United Against Injustice (UAI) and the Innocence Network. I've worked with Christian groups, too, such as Nancy Goudie's Spiritual Health Weekends for Women, and I've addressed some church groups. They were interested in hearing my Christian testimony about how God was working in my life throughout all of this adversity.

On the 2nd November 2007, Dr Michael Naughton, the founder and director of the first Innocence Project at the University of Bristol, and of the Innocence Network UK (INUK), dedicated to investigating alleged wrongful convictions, held a large conference in Bristol. Michael has always taken a strong interest in Barry's case, and we have met and spoken often. The gathering was made up of staff and students from twenty universities, together with miscarriage of justice survivors, leading experts from the CCRC, CPS and from Avon and Somerset Police. There were also some criminal barristers and representatives from HM Prison Service. The media were in evidence and they jostled amongst the known faces, including mine, as they prepared to cover the story. Barry's appeal was to start the following day, so Michael made sure I was protected from intrusion.

Hazel Keirle and I believed we'd been invited to hear the speakers, so we secured seats near the front of the auditorium, and we had just settled in when we were told our 'seats' were up on the stage. This was when we first realised that we had in fact been asked as speakers. My speech that day was one of the most hurriedly written addresses ever penned for such an event. I furiously scribbled down bullet points on a scrap of paper using a blunt eyebrow pencil, both of which I'd unearthed from the bottom of my chaotic handbag.

Since that time, I've also spoken with students for Professor Julie Price at Cardiff University. Her students were preparing submissions to the CCRC on behalf of a client, and the evidence against him was almost identical to the gunshot residue evidence in Barry's case. I'm pleased to say they eventually won this man's release.

I still address students at the University of Portsmouth, for Marika Henneberg, senior lecturer, and leader of the Criminal Justice Clinic. Some of her students take a Miscarriage of Justice module as part of their studies, and they are always shocked by what passed for justice in Barry's case. This is not the law they have been taught.

More TV interviews took place during these intervening years, with the BBC, ITV and Sky News being the main channels to request updates from me. I've chatted with many people who worked in these organisations. They would often say they were unsure of Barry's claim to be innocent, but they were always, always very respectful to me. It was clear, though, that there was a very deep rawness amongst Jill's friends and colleagues. Arriving at the ITV studio not long after the conviction, I was informed that a well-known presenter did not want to interview me. Talking to me about the murder of his close friend would have been too painful for him. John Stapleton took the place of Eamonn Holmes on GMTV Today that morning.

On another occasion, a female presenter came into the studio as I was being made ready in hair and make-up for yet another GMTV Today interview. Lorraine Kelly wasn't the person scheduled to speak with me but she was someone I had always admired and so, without thinking, I thrust out my hand to shake hers. It was only when I saw the look of alarm on her face that I realised she didn't know what to do. Was she shocked at being asked to shake hands with the sister of the man who'd been convicted of killing her friend? Her professionalism won over, and she took my hand.

Both Eamonn Holmes and Lorraine Kelly are consummate professionals; but they had lost a colleague, a friend, someone they held dear. I could never hold it against either of them for their reaction, it was perfectly understandable. It surprised and pleased me though, just how many media professionals revealed to me that they believed Barry was innocent.

14

Bereaved

As always, whenever there was an upcoming event in the Barry saga things really became arduous back home in Cork, but in 2007 this was unprecedented. Not only was my home life being disrupted by all the phone calls and media attention, but my work life was as well. I needed to speak with so many people in the run up to this new appeal. The CCRC had, at last, referred Barry's case back to the Court of Appeal, so it was vital for me to be in contact with his legal team, also with Mum and with Surjit Singh Clair from MOJO. I kept getting phone calls at work that just couldn't wait till later. There was so much to organise and my adrenaline was in overdrive; it was frenetic.

Barry had a new legal team. He had engaged this new solicitor after the early failed appeals. He had seen an advertisement in the prison publication Inside Times describing Jeremy Moore as a miscarriages of justice solicitor. Jeremy had then engaged junior barrister Geoffrey Samuels and they secured the services of William Clegg QC for the appeal. This did worry me a bit, because this case was so complex. Did this new legal team have all the information they needed, I wondered? After all, they were not at the initial trial or the first appeal. They had access to trial transcripts, of course, but we had the experience of sitting in the courtroom, and of the behind-the-scenes conversations with medical and legal people which could prove vital. Everything had to be perfect. We could not afford to lose this appeal.

Having changed jobs four years ago, I was now working in a customer service capacity in a call centre. Taking queries and sorting issues for customers was busy and demanding. From the time I arrived at work until the time I left, I was attached to my phone station by a headset, an umbilical between the customer and me and, in turn, the utility service provider I worked for. When attached, I, the individual did not exist. I was an extension of the collective, a part of the machine. Everything was monitored by the computer: how many comfort breaks were taken, how many times 'away from desk' was used as your availability status. All would have to be explained at the next appraisal. It felt as if only a machine, with its pre-set times and functions, would be efficient enough for management. Needless to say, people want to speak with people, so companies have to employ them, but then they try to operate them like interactive software. In this frenetic environment, the individual is expendable. A new group of recruits can easily be groomed to take the place of those who do not perform proficiently.

In January 2007, during the run up to the appeal, I was having to disconnect from my work station three or four times a day to deal with calls on my mobile about the upcoming legal case. The company were sympathetic and gave their permission, but I was beginning to feel an atmosphere around me. There was a change in attitude towards me that made me fear for my job. Since my family needed my wages just to stay afloat, it was a huge worry to think I may lose my job because I had to continue this fight for justice. Thankfully, I confronted the situation early and this didn't come to pass, but it did make me very aware that I must be extra conscientious about my work.

It was February 2007, and Pat still could not seem to shift the nasty flu virus that had struck us all down over Christmas. The children and I had recovered, but Pat was still very much under the weather and a bit grey around the gills. We teased him about 'man flu' and thought he might need a tonic to help him perk up. Pat had recently taken on a new job and was learning a new set of skills and routines and he was struggling with this. He'd been a diligent worker all his life, so he didn't like having to take time off work to recover, but this time it was out of his hands. He simply could not work.

With Pat on sick pay, it became even more imperative that my job remained secure. I was working extra hours whenever I could get them just to make up for the loss of income. However, Pat's job paid well, so we felt confident we'd soon catch up again when he went back . . . only he never went back. His general malaise became a debilitation, and headaches and vomiting joined the symptoms.

It first became obvious to me that something was seriously amiss with Pat when he was driving me to work at ESB Networks in Wilton.

"Pat, why haven't you taken the filter lane, honey? It's clear."

I wouldn't normally question Pat's driving. He drove for a living and was a good driver, but I was becoming concerned. This was not the first time I had noticed him crawl along in the busy middle lane when our left-turn filter was available.

"Oh, no reason, I'm just about to."

I let it go at that, but I made a mental note to watch for other signs of strange behaviour. Maybe he was more ill than I had realised.

Over the next few days, I noticed that Pat would search for something but not be able to locate it even though it was in plain view. He would open a cupboard door and not close it, then walk into it and bang his head. He could bump into things, or fall over poor Casey, our dog. Some mornings I noticed bits of broken glass strewn around the kitchen floor where the dog might step on it, but nobody knew where it had come from . . . no one was owning up! *Pat must have sight problems*, I thought. *I'd better take him for an eye examination.*

"Your sight is still 20:20, Mr Diskin, the glasses you have are quite adequate," Dee, the lady at Specsavers reported, waving us off. "We'll send out a date for your next appointment in a year. Bye, have a good day." As usual, Pat and Dee were laughing at one of Pat's jokes. I was surprised at the result of the test, but relieved. There was no degenerative eye condition . . . maybe Pat just needed more rest.

On a trip to the doctor, Pat was given an injection to stop the sickness, along with painkillers. He was told that it should solve things, but to come back if anything got worse. I'd been monitoring him from work, which had meant more time away from the phone, but when he called to say he felt worse, I phoned for an immediate appointment with the GP surgery.

"You get yourself ready, Pat, and I'll collect you shortly. I'm just leaving work, they've given me the time off to take you back to the doctor."

The supervisor on duty had said to go straight away. "You can make up the time later, Michelle." She looked at me a little strangely, probably wondering why I needed to ask since it seemed to be an emergency, but my mind was under such intense pressure that I couldn't think clearly.

"Right, I'll go then . . ." In my brain I closed off the mental compartment where I stored work-related issues, and reopened the one for home and family.

Arriving home, feeling somewhat flustered after leaving work early, I was surprised to see Pat sitting in his armchair, not prepared for going.

"Pat, you didn't get ready for your appointment, and it's in ten minutes," I called out anxiously, hanging up my keys on the rack. "Will you be ready soon?"

Pat looked really dishevelled. He had not shaved, showered, or even changed his clothes. This was not the Pat I'd lived with for almost twenty five years. That man would have been spick and span for a doctor's visit, no matter what. He'd never have gone looking like this!

"I'm okay as I am," he barked at me. I backed off and pretended to do something else. A few minutes later, I let him know it was time to go.

"Pat, look at your shoes!" I stared aghast at my husband. He had just put mismatched shoes on the wrong feet.

"They're fine," he shot back.

The deep-seated urge to fix it for him, to make everything normal and as it should be, overwhelmed me. However, I knew in my heart that this was something the doctor needed to see, so I did not intervene. I got Pat into the car and we drove off.

"Michael, did you see him?" Dr Michael Crotty, who had been our family doctor for years, had come into the reception area just as I was ushering Pat into the waiting room. "I left him like that, Michael," I said under my breath, "so you could see how poor he is."

A look passed between us, knowing and sad and with no need of words. This was not the Pat we both knew.

"Hi ya Pat, I'm sending you straight to the hospital for an x-ray, buddy. There's no need for an appointment, you go right away. They're expecting you." I looked at Pat for signs of panic, but he seemed not to have appreciated the implications.

The Accident & Emergency Department was overflowing with people needing attention, and Pat was put onto a trolley along a corridor. There was no privacy here for anyone. Elderly people, young children, male and female, all waited here for a decision from a doctor. Pat was no different. The nursing staff were stretched to breaking point as I sat beside Pat for long hours. He lay on the unyielding trolley, sometimes speaking to me, but often just lying there with his eyes closed. I thought he was sleeping. Unidentifiable people floated by in the corridor as we waited for answers. Then someone came from the x-ray department and, finding Pat sleeping, said to me, "We've found a shadow on the brain scan. We're quite concerned." Immediately, Pat's eyes flew open. He had not been sleeping at all, just blocking out the need to talk to anyone.

Events became hazy after this. I know we saw a surgeon and he told Pat he had a tumour. I know we had to tell the family about the upcoming surgery . . . but the hardest of all was when we sat the children down to try to explain it to them. Pat was just 51, and so healthy in every other way. This news was hard to take in.

The surgery went well, with 85% of the tumour being removed, and Pat's recovery was extraordinary. He was sitting up in bed and cracking jokes with visitors and staff, so much so that he had to be moved to a private room for a few days before going home to give other recovering patients some much needed peace and quiet!

On one visit to the 'comedy room' he'd been banished to, Pat regaled us with talk of fairies, or as he put it: "There are angels dancing on the end of my bed." He was laughing, but at pains to point out that they really were there, dancing. He seemed very happy to see them. We just thought it must be the invasive nature of brain surgery, but I did say a prayer of thanks for how this vision had encouraged Pat. Shortly after this, Pat was well enough to be discharged and we took him home to continue his recovery.

My work for Barry now ceased. Nothing mattered except Pat and this insidious illness. It was as though we had woken up together in a bubble, and no one could join us there. This was the biggest challenge of our marriage and it became our whole world, our focus. We were now sharing something profoundly intimate: mortality. We talked about wills and family and putting our affairs in order, even though the surgeon had given Pat a prognosis that he might look forward to living for another two years, and that some people with the same strain of cancer had been known to live on for nine. Pat asked me many questions during this very strange and curiously insular time together, but there was one question I had real difficulty answering. With a childlike expression of fear, the fear of the unknown, Pat asked, "Michelle, can you tell me what Heaven will be like?"

What will Heaven be like? Not exactly a question posed every day. Of course, Pat knew I had attended Bible studies on many topics, but though I knew this in my heart, I couldn't find the words or, more importantly, the Biblical references to share with him.

Pat fixed me with a gaze, one I'd seen often on the faces of my children. It said, *I trust you to know, and I trust you to look after me.* This topic was very important to Pat, and it was vital that I did not gloss over it with platitudes.

"Pat, let's find someone for you to speak with, someone who has more knowledge than I."

There were many eminently knowledgeable people at Lee Valley Bible Church and Pat chose to speak with the Reverend Ernie Tromsness, a friend and former leader at the Church. As I helped Ernie's wife Nancy with lunch, the men went into another room for their discussion. When they emerged, Pat's worried frown had been replaced by a look of pure joy. He was no longer afraid, death held no sting for him!

Pat had rarely spoken about his faith with others; he was worried people might think him a bit weird. Now he made it his life's work to share with people about his Saviour, and even asked to stand in church to give a testimony. During this, he voiced the words that have been so important to me and to many others since.

"Do not wait until tomorrow to tell your wife you love her. There may not be a tomorrow."

Over the next four weeks we watched as Pat went from bad to good, then back to bad again. He was having absence seizures now, which I recognised from seeing Barry's. Our GP phoned the hospital, and although we did go to see them, they had no hope to offer us. The tumour was back, bigger than before, and it was a matter of time . . . just how little time, we couldn't know.

Just six weeks after surgery, and ten weeks since diagnosis, Pat was admitted to Cork University Hospital for the last time. It was sudden and inexplicable. How could this have happened? We had to scramble to get everyone to the hospital to say goodbye. Pat was lucid a lot of the time and able to hold short conversations, with the steroids holding back the pain of the swelling. He knew what was happening and said his goodbyes, too. He died in a quiet private room at 1am on Friday April 27th, 2007.

Later, I noted that it was one day after the seventh anniversary of Jill Dando's death. I was glad they would not share the same date, though we would never forget hers, either.

In the days after Pat's passing I felt as though my brain would not function. My synaptic pathways seemed to be blocked, and just trying to walk was like trudging through treacle wearing heavy boots. Funerals in Ireland are held just two days after death unless there is a good reason, such as an autopsy, or important relatives journeying from far away. Ours had no grounds for delay so we waked Pat at home after an evening service of prayer, then held the funeral, more a celebration of life, in Ardfallen Methodist Church near Douglas in Cork. There were hundreds of people present to say their goodbyes to this very popular man. Pat's words about love were read out and we saw them have a profound effect on those gathered. He would have been so gratified to know this.

My own grief was put on hold. There was just so much to do, so many people to see. Registering the death was a shock, though the people in Births Deaths & Marriages in Cork City were so understanding. I was led to a private room and left with forms to sign. Looking them over after I'd signed, the registrar said, "I'm so sorry, Mrs Diskin, but you're not Pat's wife anymore. You must write 'widow' in here."

I felt I had lost something of myself. My identity as a wife for almost twenty-five years was gone. I was now a widow, and I didn't know how to be one of those.

Stress and tension in my upper body had, over the years, resulted in breast lumps which had to be checked or biopsied, and this tension was at its highest during 2007. After the funeral when I found a lump in my breast again, I didn't feel I could confide in anyone because everyone was still raw after losing Pat. When I did go back to the breast clinic at CUH, I became extremely upset and poured out all my fears and pain to the consultant. On hearing that I had just buried my husband, he put me in the personal care of a nurse. "Please get Mrs Diskin a cup of tea and stay with her for a while, she can't drive home alone in such distress."

Thank you, Professor Redmond, for being so understanding, and for cheering me up by wearing such outlandish bow-ties and brightly coloured jackets. They're much more fun than scrubs.

Driving Mum back to the airport after her visit for the funeral, I felt sorry she was leaving, but I also felt glad. I had not been able to grieve. Mum had to sleep in my bed with me because the children were all at home and we didn't have a spare bed. Of course, this meant I couldn't let my feelings out in private. There was simply no privacy. I knew I would have to do so soon, or burst.

When I arrived back from the airport, all the children were out. Opening my front door, I suddenly felt it all well up inside me, like a volcano ready to erupt. I ran into the front room with Casey in tow and fell onto the brown leather couch. There, I howled out my grief and pain in deep hot sobs, scaring the poor dog, who put his head on my lap to comfort me.

15

2007 Appeal

The wheels of justice ground inexorably on, and Barry's second appeal was set to be heard in November of 2007. The world would not stop turning just because we were in mourning.

There was a major change with this appeal. The FDR evidence and how it had been presented to the jury at trial had been discredited, because the finding of one particle could not prove that he *had* done it, nor show that he *hadn't*. It could not help the court at all; it was completely neutral. We had found this out by chance. Two forensic scientists, one of them the prosecution's expert witness Robin Keeley, were discussing the evidence not long after the conviction, and how the FDR had been wrongly interpreted by the prosecution. They decided to test the evidence and arrived at the conclusion that the FDR proved neutral. Unfortunately for Barry, they did nothing with this finding until, in 2006, this conversation was communicated to a CCRC officer who was at the Forensic Science Service on other business. Without this chance communication, Barry would probably still be waiting for 'new' evidence so he could appeal.

The FDR, a microscopic particle, which was said at trial to be a match to the residue found on the victim's head, need not even have come from a gun. It could also have come from a firework, an airbag in a car, or other sources. It was not unique. Two jury members from the 2001 trial were very unhappy about this evidence and they said this in a Panorama documentary in 2006.

Juror Janet Herbert had first come forward within days of the conviction. She had tried to contact Mansfield via the Old Bailey to say she was extremely disturbed by irregularities within the jury's deliberations. Although we had known about this at the time, we were unable to do anything about it, because it was against the law for her to try to speak to the defendant's legal team. This juror had to live with her unease until 2006, when Raphael Rowe and the Panorama team traced her for their documentary, *Jill Dando's Murder: The New Evidence*. The possibility of prison was still there for her, but she was eager to tell her story.

"I think it was the strongest piece of evidence the police had against Mr George. It came over that this was definitely the particle that came from the gun that killed Miss Dando, and the particle was in his coat." Janet Herbert spoke further about her concerns with the jury process. She said that at the hotel they'd been sent to overnight, some jurors broke away and formed a small group. They discussed the case, which the judge had expressly told them not to, and she and others were excluded. Then she felt intimidated to agree with their decision.

The foreman of the jury also spoke to the Panorama team, but wished to remain anonymous. He declared, "I think it was one of the foundations of the prosecution case. I think without that the case would have failed . . . it was put across at trial that it linked him to the crime."

The CCRC said that on this basis, the particle evidence should never have been admitted at trial.

As we approached the first day of this new appeal, there was the usual flurry of newspaper and TV coverage of the case. I was back in England to attend the proceedings when I saw this inflammatory headline in the Daily Mail. It made me almost breathless with anger:

Blonde psychologist paid £500 a day to give Dando Killer head massages in his cell.

The front page carried a large photo of Dr Young. Outraged cannot adequately describe the feelings I had on seeing this. Firstly, 'Dando Killer'? Barry was fighting for justice because he was not Jill's killer. Next, what had this eminent psychologist's gender or hair colour to do with her job or professionalism? I didn't see any headlines of this nature written towards Dr Gisli Gudjonsson, and he is also blond. This lack of respect would never have been levelled at a man.

Then there is the head massaging. Whose vivid imagination did this ooze from? Barry is a disabled man, he needed extra help to function and to understand what was happening in the court. The court recognised that and the media ridiculed it. This was reckless and disrespectful journalism and it was used to inflame the public against Barry.

Infuriated, I arrived at court on the first day of the appeal waving a copy of this offending publication. I communicated to the waiting journalists exactly what I thought of this atrocious and deceitful reporting – all of them recorded my words, all took photos, but no one printed anything.

After Barry had been convicted in 2001, there were many news articles written by people expressing their own take on the case. Nick Ross of Crimewatch was no exception, but even in my befuddled, post-conviction dejection, I could not miss the absurdity of this headline in the News of the World:

"I always knew it was Barry George, or someone like him!"

If it had been 'someone like him', would that have been justification for imprisoning Barry George? Ross had always intimated that he had insider information from the police that proved the conviction was right, even going so far as to try to interfere with the due process of the court. He wrote a letter to the three high court judges who were presiding over Barry's 2007 appeal. They were Lord Chief Justice Lord Phillips, Lord Justice Leveson and Mr Justice Simon Read. All of the evidence before the court had been provided by the

CCRC, and was the only reason this case was being referred back to the Court of Appeal.

Ross wrote, "Your Lordships, I am not sure of the propriety of writing to you, but you cannot have been blind to the barrage of publicity claiming Barry George is innocent . . ."

It was a long letter. I recall one of the judges informing the court that they had received it, but had deliberately not read it. Ross, though, had prepared for this eventuality. He had distributed the letter to any newspaper group that would publish it. Personally, I cannot conceive of anybody being so disrespectful to the courts, and to three high court judges, that they would seek to blackmail them into seeing things their way. No matter how upset Ross had been at the killing of his Crimewatch co-presenter, no matter what he *thought* he knew, he was trying to pervert the course of justice, and the judges were incensed.

Before the appeal, Barry's legal team had explained to us that the best thing that could happen for Barry, if his conviction was quashed, was a retrial. If the judges called for one, they would not contest it because it would show once and for all that the other evidence was worthless. It would also show he had not 'got off on a technicality'.

The evidence was impartially reviewed and Barry was acquitted. In the summing up of the Court of Appeal's decision, Lord Phillips said . . .

"It is impossible to know what weight, if any, the jury attached to the FDR evidence. It is equally impossible to know what verdict they would have reached had they been told, as we were told, by the witnesses who gave evidence before us, that it was just as likely that the single particle of FDR came from some extraneous source as it was that it came from a gun fired by the appellant. The verdict is unsafe. The conviction will be quashed."

The judges called for a re-trial.

16

Retrial

Being back in Court One was a painful reminder of what had happened in our lives all those years ago. I truly hoped that this time, all would be put right. In the months leading up to the trial, I had received many emails from Jeremy Moore asking for assistance with facts and, strangely, discussing probation and what would happen if and when Barry was freed. Hazel was a bit concerned when I asked if this was right.

"No, it's not right, Michelle, only offenders go to probation. Barry will be seen by another agency as a miscarriage of justice if he's found not guilty. Maybe you should just ring Jeremy and say this."

This happened a few times, and each time I reminded Jeremy that probation was not needed. A few weeks before the trial I was contacted by someone from the Miscarriage of Justice Support Services (MJSS).

"Hello Michelle, my name is Carla Frégiste Moore, and I will be Barry's case worker if he's is freed at retrial. Basically, our organisation was set up to help people who were wrongly convicted to restart their lives. We make sure they have a bank account, that they get any benefits back on stream, find accommodation and the like. I'll be going to visit Barry very soon to ascertain his needs. I thought I'd introduce myself to you, too, so you know what's happening."

This was good news. It seems that the CCRC contact the MJSS whenever there's a chance of an acquittal. This call was very timely and Carla was very helpful, so when I was summoned to a meeting with Barry's legal team on my own, I asked Carla to accompany me as my friend and advocate. I felt the need for support, as these men were a force, and I was afraid of being browbeaten despite them being Barry's legal team. I felt they disapproved of me, and only wanted me involved to keep Barry calm. Carla's presence had a neutralising effect on the dynamic of this meeting, and I managed to get my points across.

The single blue/grey cloth fibre rose up again at the retrial. Not only was it resurrected, it was given all the prominence of the discredited FDR evidence from the first trial. It became a giant. I sat listening in shock as the new prosecutor, Jonathan Laidlaw QC who had been the assistant in the first trial, tried to show that this fibre could have come from no other source than the defendant. Cross-examination by the defence team revealed that no samples had been taken from any of the police who, necessarily, tramped all over the crime scene, or from ambulance personnel who attended to the victim, nor from witnesses who discovered the body. Sampling was not carried out on Alan Farthing's clothing, who was Ms Dando's fiancé. This should have been done to eliminate the fibre from the case or investigate possible innocent contamination. Incredulously, I heard that no samples were taken from Jill's own wardrobe either, to be certain this wasn't from her own clothing!

The defence team found themselves asking the very same question Mansfield had asked: if Barry had worn his woollen coat at the scene of the murder, where were the readily shed fibres from that?

Many people from the original trial were called by the police to give their evidence again at this retrial. Three of them were personnel from the HAFAD centre. At the first trial, these witnesses had given conflicting evidence of their recollections of the time Barry had been in the office on the day of the murder. Now, amazingly, they had each reassessed their timings. I listened in awe to the testimony, as each one gave their reason for their initial incorrect reporting of these times. Each one now testified that Barry would have been in the centre at 11:50!

Their evidence showed what Susan Bicknell's testimony had shown all along, that it was impossible for Barry to have been in Gowan Avenue at the time the murder took place.

The law changed in 2003, allowing evidence of previous convictions to be put before the jury, thus allowing the prosecution to cite these as evidence of the defendant's bad character.

I had known of Barry's two convictions in 1983, but I was shocked to hear the 'bad character' evidence. The court was told how Barry would follow women in the street, photographing them without their knowledge, and the way he made some women feel very frightened. They were also informed of how he impersonated a police officer back in the 80s, and his many fantasies. It was hard to sit and listen to all of this. The women who had been scared related incidents that would have caused me to feel the same . . . was this really my brother? I'd been out of his life for so many years that I hadn't understood what his life had become.

The jury was further informed by the prosecutor that Barry's behaviour on the day of Jill's murder and in the following days was indicative of guilt. Yet, with no corroborating evidence from the murder scene and no motive, how was this proof?

There is no doubt that Barry's behaviour has been bizarre and unacceptable, but it was normal for him. Forming relationships is a challenge for most people on the autism spectrum, although this can't absolve him of responsibility for his actions. Barry always looks suspicious; he stands out like a sore thumb, and he can't see this himself. We have had many discussions on this and we've had many sessions to try to help him become more organised, to no avail. I've realised that subtlety and beating about the bush don't work when trying to help him recognise where the issues lie; any advice has to be clear and concise. Families dealing with Asperger's Syndrome in their midst will recognise this need for clarity. His hoarding compulsion is not just evident in his muddled home, but also on his person, as he carries around no end of items that he 'might need', but never really will.

Also, Barry doesn't view his lies as untruths, but as exaggerations. Many people lie and build themselves up, especially in job interviews and on CVs, but Barry so badly wants to look important in the eyes of others that he comes across as a fantasist. The difference is that he does not believe his own fabrications, he just wants others to, and can't recognise that they can often see the truth and think he's strange. Another trait he and I have discussed, if my nagging at him can be described as a discussion, is his propensity to get aggravated for seemingly small things. I say seemingly, because these upsets are important to him at that time. His actions at HAFAD on the day of the murder demonstrate this characteristic.

There's great sadness for me in writing about all of this. This man is the little brother I grew up with, until we lost contact after I left the UK in 1973. I believe he should never have gone to live alone at the tender age of sixteen; he needed so much more guidance, which he missed out on due to the fractured condition of our family and the lack of understanding about his condition. Autistic tendencies are always challenging, and for a family trying to deal with these challenges without any knowledge or support, it can be overwhelming. All too many youngsters have ended up in our courts and our prisons. Barry fell through the cracks, and it is too late to put preventative measures in place or educational supports to teach him constructive communication skills. Thankfully today there is more understanding of how to support people after a diagnosis. The difficulty for many families may be in getting that initial diagnosis. Specific help for families with how to understand and manage the communication problems is helpful, too. I wish this had been available to us and to Barry growing up.

It's not easy for people who live with an invisible disability, that feeling of being on the outside, not quite fitting in. Our sister Susan also experienced huge challenges because she shared many of the same life-limiting impediments. Being asked to look after both of them as we grew up was extremely demanding on me as a child, but for some reason I always felt it was right, it was my responsibility. I recognised, too, that I could well have been born disabled. There but for the grace of God, go I.

Barry's family and friends accept and love him just the way he is, but it's important to point out that we do not condone his bad behaviour. Wrong is still wrong, and he must accept responsibility for his past and future actions.

Of course, none of this bad character evidence was capable of placing him at a murder scene with a modified gun in his hand. That was all smoke and mirrors by the prosecution. It merely exposed Barry's shambolic life, not any predisposition to kill.

Sometimes I just couldn't face another encounter with the media at break time. It was like living in a goldfish bowl. So instead of going to the canteen, I would sit on the benches outside of the courtroom and try to read a book. About a week into the retrial, a man approached me carrying a green document folio and some papers in his hand. He was tallish, slim and wearing casual dress; light coloured trousers and a pale blue jumper. Obviously he was not attached to the proceedings in the courtroom, so I assumed he was a journalist, and kept my eyes cast downward so as not to encourage him with eye contact.

"Hello, you are Barry's sister, aren't you?"

Oh no, I thought. *Here we go again.*

"Barry's counsel asked me to chat with you about what happens if your brother is found not guilty." He stood, waiting for my response.

"Oh, in what way?" I answered, probably a bit sharply. "Sorry, who are you again?" This conversation seemed a bit odd to me. He looked rather perplexed at my abruptness.

"I'm from the probation service, and I'll be Barry's probation officer . . ." I stopped him, mid-sentence, shock and disbelief on my face.

"I'm really sorry, and I don't know why you've been sent to speak with me, but if Barry is released at the end of this trial he will be a miscarriage of justice and will come under the MJSS, not probation," I fired back at him. I remember thinking, *what the heck is going on here?*

"Oh, really? Yes, yes, I don't know why I was sent either, it must have been a mistake." He backed away, looking even more perplexed.

When I challenged Barry's legal team, they indicated that it must have been an error on someone's part. They did not say they'd sent him and denied all knowledge of it.

The trial continued, but I found the legal team quite hostile towards me, unless they were having problems with Barry, then it was, "When you visit him in Belmarsh, can you try to talk sense to him, try to make him understand?" This would have been because Barry thought they should do A when they thought B, or vice versa. Mansfield had also had these same issues, but he had handled them in a different manner.

It seemed as though they needed me, but wished I wasn't there; I was a fly in the ointment. I had had this issue right from the start, when Barry first changed his solicitor. I think it was because I asked too many questions and tracked their each and every move. For them, this was a job, and they'd go home to tea if Barry was convicted again. For me, this was my brother's life, our lives. It was a huge injustice already, let alone if he went back to prison.

The retrial was drawing to a close, and it was time for the summing up of the two sides. I really hoped enough had been done to ensure a not guilty verdict, as I had no idea what to do next otherwise.

Before the jury foreman gave the verdict, though, the judge had asked that everyone sit down and stay in their seats. He knew that the media, who were present in court, would be anxious to be the first to get the verdict out to their offices and would run out to phone them immediately. He didn't want anyone to disrupt the court's proceedings with scuffling and door banging. I'd seen this before, too, at the first trial.

"This is difficult enough for the jury, don't make it harder for them," he said, looking sombre.

My heart sank at those words, and I held on even tighter to the hands of my friends from MOJO. The words seemed to herald a negative verdict for us. Barry and I had been preparing ourselves for another guilty verdict because we didn't dare not to. After all, we had been there before, and Barry should not have been found guilty that time, either.

17

The Verdict

"We find the defendant not guilty."

YES! It was a unanimous verdict. I jumped out of my seat and punched the air with both hands. For the last eight years, I had kept my emotions locked away from the public gaze, but not today. Today, the whole world would be allowed to see. I did not hide my elation. This was what we'd worked so long for.

Thank you, God. Thank you, thank you, thank you!

Catching the eye of a jury member, I couldn't resist mouthing 'thank you' to him, too. I wanted those twelve men and women to know how much I appreciated what they had done. They had brought our eight year nightmare to an end. *Alleluia and praise the Lord.* My heart was bubbling over with joy.

Poor Barry looked incredulous and lost, standing in the dock. It was obvious he didn't know what to do next. He looked over to the door leading from the dock into the court, but no one unlocked it for him. The bolt was on our side and now I wish I'd been more courageous.

The judge declared, "Mr George is entitled to be treated as an innocent man." Yet, he wasn't allowed to leave the court by the courtroom door like all the other free men and women. He had to be led away from the dock and back down the narrow concrete stairs to the cells to be processed out, to sign papers and such, and we couldn't go with him. We couldn't even hug him, but my disappointment at this was tempered only with the knowledge that we would be together soon, and that nobody could take him away from us after that.

He was accompanied by Dr Young, who had been his rock throughout these years. She had sat with him in the dock, making sure that he was able to follow all the court's proceedings. She kept a running note of everything so he could refer to it if he'd missed it.

Jeremy Moore, Geoffrey Samuels and William Clegg, the three men who made up his legal team, also left the court to go with him. There was another man there, too, but I didn't know him and presumed he was from Jeremy's law firm. Hazel Keirle had wanted to be in court with me, but circumstances made that impossible. Instead, Tania Davis, her daughter, accompanied me to court each day so I'd never feel alone. Surj Singh Clair came when he could. He had his own business in PR, but volunteered those skills to MOJO, pro bono. Thankfully, Mike was also in court that day. We exited Court One for the very last time and waited about in the hallowed halls of the Old Bailey, having asked Jeremy to ring one of our mobiles whenever they needed us, and when Barry was ready to leave. Then I turned my attention to what was going on around me.

An absolute frenzy was taking place within the vicinity of Court One. There were phone calls and text messages coming in on everyone's phones; it was bedlam. I had calls and texts from Britain, Ireland and as far away as Spain, where friends of ours were watching Spanish TV while on holiday. They could not understand the Spanish newscast, so they were texting to find out what had happened and if it was good news!

Mostly the messages were of congratulations. Others were media personnel seeking the 'exclusive' interview with Barry. Friends rallied around to protect me from the scrum, forming a human barrier to stop intruders reaching me. My two mobiles had calls on them, simultaneously, one on my UK mobile and one on my Irish one. Family and friends in Ireland were clamouring for information and cheering and jumping up and down. I thought of how ecstatic Pat would have been if he'd been alive to share in this. He'd have been outside the front door with our neighbours, receiving back-claps and crying tears of joy and relief, but of course, he wasn't here to share in our celebrations. In the midst of all this happiness, there was a sting in my heart. How I wished he were still here to give me the congratulatory hug I so needed to feel, to take his place beside me and share in our joy.

Both phones were bleeping and vibrating constantly as new messages came in. I had to ignore incoming calls so I could ring Mum with the good news before she heard it on TV. I'm fairly sure there were journalists outside of her home within minutes, but she wasn't answering her front door.

"Mum, he's free! Not guilty! Mum, can you hear me?" It was actually me who couldn't hear her; there was just so much going on around me.

"Is he coming home?" she asked, but I didn't know what to tell her.

"I don't know what's going to happen, Mum. We weren't expecting a decision today and so no one has thought that far ahead. I'll ring again shortly to let you know what's happening."

During this crazy time, another mobile was thrust under my nose. "You need to take this, Michelle." It was a journalist, and he handed me his phone.

"Who is it?" I mouthed, wondering where I would find another hand to take this phone, and another ear to listen to it.

"It's Paddy Hill," he mouthed back. "He wants to speak with you."

Because there were people hovering nearby trying to catch every word of any conversation I was having, I had to take this guy's phone away. I went to the stairwell, being careful I didn't lose the signal. Paddy sounded as though he was laughing and crying at the same time. He kept saying, "Well done you! You did it." As was his way, this was liberally sprinkled with expletives as he shared his joy and anger. "Eight f***ing years! Will this so-called justice system ever f***ing learn?!" There's no way I could share *all* of Paddy's scathing comments here, but I loved him for it. Paddy is such an inspiration.

This day was a day of mixed emotions, a time of elation and frustration, of joy and tears. Joy, that we had finally received justice.

Tears, for the unnecessarily lost years and the pain and the suffering we had all endured because our loved one had been convicted of a murder he didn't commit.

The four of us waited upstairs in the canteen on the second floor for a phone call from Jeremy to say we could come and collect Barry and take him home. We'd been waiting now for probably an hour. Could there be a problem? It was inconceivable that we could have been forgotten.

Hearing a flurry of activity outside in the street, we each craned our necks to see what was going on below, giving up when we realised we couldn't see the front door area from our window because we were directly above it. Anyway, that had to be for another case. Barry and his team knew where we were, they wouldn't give an official statement to the media without me being there. Barry wanted me to give a statement on behalf of his family. We settled down again with our paper cups of cold coffee from the vending machine, and waited on.

"This is just crazy," I said after another stultifying half hour with no contact. "We have to go down and see if someone can find the legal team, it can't possibly take this long to process someone out." At this stage I wished we'd protested against Barry being processed out and had taken him directly from the dock, even if officials didn't like it, but our respect for the court prevented us.

Having sat for so long in the uninspiring canteen, it was a relief to finally be moving again. We took the stairs instead of the lift to stretch our leg muscles, and headed for the security desk on the ground floor. I was surprised that we had been able to sit for that long, anyway, with the amount of adrenalin we had built up.

Arriving at the security area where we'd spent so much time waiting to gain access to the trial, I asked a guard if he could find out what was happening. Surely it couldn't take this long?

He walked us to the doorway where I had often observed the legals disappearing, going down to the bowels of the building to see their clients in the cells. As we drew nearer, the door opened, and a very dapper-looking William Clegg emerged from it. He had changed from his silks, and was now wearing an unusual suit in an oatmeal colour. Some part of my mind registered that it was double breasted and without collar and lapels, which certainly gave it a uniquely distinguished look, even if it was a tad unflattering on a man of his girth. Here was the man to whom I owed a huge debt of gratitude so, thrusting out my hand, I sought to shake his as I verbalised my thanks. I hadn't had a chance to speak with him since the verdict.

"Where have you been?" was the barked response to my proffered hand. "We've been looking for you everywhere. You disappeared."

He looked down at my outstretched hand like he wasn't sure he wanted to touch it. I received a grudging and cursory handshake from this man, whose face was like thunder, but I reached around to hug him anyway. I was so happy to see him and to tell him how grateful I was. What on earth could be the problem?

"Bill, we all have our phones turned on, and not one of us received a call from you," I tried to explain, since he clearly thought we'd been remise. "We told Jeremy we'd be up in the canteen because we needed to get away from the media. There are no missed calls . . ."

"This way," he snapped, "just family." He cast a furious look towards Surj and Tania. I looked to my MOJO friends, the people who had been my support for so long, but they shooed us off.

"Go! We'll wait outside for you, you can ring if you need anything," Tania smiled reassuringly. Grabbing her in a quick hug, I turned away and, with Mike, followed the inexplicably angry QC through the door and into uncharted corridors. As we walked through the long passageways, I tried to garner some more information from Mr Clegg.

"Is everything alright?" I asked him. "We waited to hear from you but nobody rang." It was obvious I wasn't going to get a response, just the thunderous look. Struggling to keep up, I determined that nothing would be allowed to spoil this day for us. It was our day of triumph, after all, and long fought for.

He ushered us into a room to our left. It seemed to be about 12 foot by 10, and was dark and dingy, very poorly illuminated. There was only one small window, high up in the wall at the end. There was another room adjoining this one and the door was ajar, but I couldn't see into it, though I could hear people speaking in there. At the end the room, sitting down, was a very tired, confused and frightened-looking Barry. I rushed to him, gripping him in a huge bear hug. Also in this room, along with Mr Clegg and Mike, was the man I didn't know. Five people in one very small room. Dr Young and Jeremy joined us from the other room. The enormity of the occasion threatened to engulf me and I still couldn't take the cheesy grin off my face. *He's free!*

Okay, what now? I thought. *Do I take him home to Mum's place, or to somewhere else?* I'd considered the possibilities for this day for such a long time, but it was impossible to put firm plans into place for something that may or may not happen, and with no date to work with. We obviously couldn't predict when the jury would come back with their verdict, so I just needed a few minutes to relax and think, then I'd work something out. My mind started to formulate a plan. Probably we'll have to go to a hotel, then . . .

A thunderous voice interrupted my thoughts. "Where were you? We couldn't get hold of you. We didn't know what to do with him. A taxi will be here in a minute to take him to a bail hostel. He can't go home to his mother's, it'll be mobbed. The taxi is on its way and he's going . . ."

"What?" That woke me from my reverie. "A bail hostel? No, you can't be serious. We were here all the time, we hadn't left the building. No one called us!" I was shaking my head in an effort to make sense of this.

"It's all arranged now. If you have a better idea, you'd better tell us. We couldn't find you. What's *your* plan, then? You're the one who's controlling everything, tell us what you're going to do with him. The taxi will be here any minute, what are we supposed to do?"

On and on it went, banging into my head till I felt like I'd been in the ring with Mike Tyson. I tried talking, tried explaining that

I just needed a moment to think. I wasn't ungrateful, but I hadn't received the expected call. The tirade went on and on. I could see what made this man so effective in court; I felt battered.

Dear God, I prayed silently, *I just need time to form coherent thoughts. Please, Lord, please, block this man's voice out of my head so I can think. I can't even understand his anger, Lord, what did I do wrong? Oh God, I can't let Barry go to a bail hostel and . . . Lord, did he just say probation officer?* I emerged from my prayer.

"Barry won't be going to probation. Why should a probation officer be waiting to speak with him? His reintegration needs are being met by the MJSS, not by probation," I informed the haranguing voice.

"It's all arranged now, and you come in saying it's not good enough, well you'd better . . ."

I tuned him out again. There was a constricting band of pressure around my head, like someone was tightening a giant jubilee clip around my forehead. I put my head in my hands to relieve the tension. Looking up, I saw Mike standing there looking rather uncomfortable, but he had nothing to say since this tirade was aimed solely at me.

Oh, Lord. I turned again to God in prayer. *There is something terribly wrong here. I'm standing in the wrong picture! This is not the joyous scene that I should be a part of, this is another nightmare. Dear Heavenly Father, how much more can I take? Please Lord, how far can this twig bend before it breaks?*

A calmness descended on me. It made no sense: nothing had changed, the voice was still beating into me insistently, but now I knew what to do. Checking my mobile phone for a signal, I rang Barry's case worker, Carla, the woman who had come to the legal meeting with me when I'd felt the need for support, and who had visited Barry in prison so that he knew who was going to sort out his problems on release. *She'll give me sound advice,* I thought.

"Carla, they want to send Barry to a bail hostel and send in a probation officer to see him. What shall I do?"

"What?! What are they doing that for? He's not a probation client, he's a Miscarriage of Justice, and they come under the MJSS. What is all this nonsense?" Carla was astonished and obviously outraged at this.

I went on to tell her what had been arranged and she told me, in no uncertain terms, that he must not go to that hostel. Carla was as confused as I was: she'd had meetings with the legal team, and they'd known all along she was Barry's case worker. She'd visited the prison to get to know Barry and the needs he would have upon his release. She had spoken at length about the services she would provide Barry with once he was released. This service was a part of the Citizens Advice Bureau and funded by the Home Office; there was no way that any legal luminary could say he didn't know about this. The MJSS office is attached to the courts at the Royal Courts of Justice in The Strand, where Barry won his appeal.

I was being hurried again, so I ended my call to Carla. "The taxi is almost here. What is your plan? If you have a better one, what is it? He can go there for tonight." The staccato voice drilled at me. *This has got to be what brainwashing is like,* I thought. *I can barely think.*

"Can we go with him, get him settled? Can he see his Mum?" I implored. Mum hadn't even seen her son yet.

"I don't know. Come on, they're expecting him. What are you going to do?"

Was this really Barry's legal counsel being so nasty? It was hard to fathom. I pulled God's calm back around me like a life jacket thrown to a drowning man. Trying to ignore the annoyance that my noncompliance seemed to be causing, I asked for the hostel's number so I could get some information. I then typed the number that Mr Clegg gave me into my mobile and spoke to a man at the hostel. He informed me that under no circumstances could we accompany Barry to the premises, and he wouldn't be allowed to have visitors, either. It sounded as though he was to be treated as an ex-offender – this man, my brother, who had spent eight years in prison for someone else's appalling crime. A terrible mental image started to form in my befuddled brain. A picture of Barry in that awful place, surrounded and hounded by the press, not able to even look out of a window. He would be like a guilty man hiding away, effectively a prisoner again. I just couldn't let that happen.

The irate QC looked close to apoplexy, and absently, I wondered how his blood pressure was doing.

"The taxi is here," he snapped.

Oh, God, you must help us. Taking out my phone again, I rang Surj, who was waiting out at the front of the courthouse for me to come out and speak to the press.

"Surj, they want to send Barry to a bail hostel, and the cab is here to take him. I can't let them do this, but where can I take him? I have to make a decision *right now,* and I can't think. I also have to make the statement outside of the court, or it will look as if we are running away."

Surj came to my rescue. "OK, Michelle, put him in the cab but send him to my hotel. We'll take it from there."

Yes, a plan! Thank you, Lord.

"Right," I addressed the angry red face with more confidence than I felt. "We'll take the cab, but we're going to an unknown location. I'll see them all off and then go back out to the media, who are waiting for me at the front door. I can join everyone later. Mike, would you go with him, please? Then I'll know he's safe."

Mike agreed and Dr Young offered to go, too, in case it all got too much for Barry and he needed her support. I was so grateful to them both. Maybe this would turn out alright, after all.

Bundling them all into the taxi, I waved them off, but I didn't notice that the unknown man got in with them as well.

Out at the back gate of the Old Bailey, I could see one lone cameraman who snapped through the cab's windows as they escaped the confines of the yard. He's safe now, God go with them.

Escape was not as straightforward for me. I still had one more ordeal before I could join them all for a well-deserved celebration, and maybe recapture some of the joy that this long-awaited day had heralded. Offering up a heartfelt prayer, I turned to retrace my steps through the hallowed halls of the Old Bailey, and back to the front door.

"You can't come back in here, you have to go around." Mr Clegg was standing inside the building, refusing me entry.

What's he talking about? I've just taken two steps back inside of the building that I came out of, of course I can go back! Maybe he doesn't understand why I must go this way, my overloaded brain reasoned. I explained that I needed to get back to the front of the courthouse to make the family's speech to the media, that they were all waiting for me.

"You're not allowed back in here," he said again. He still looked peeved, and he used his bulk to block my way forward. Turning to what I thought to be two security guards, not five yards away, who were witnessing this conversation, he waved an arm at them and said, "They won't let you back into the building, you have to go that way." He pointed out through the back door, but at nothing in particular.

I could see by the officers' body language that this was disingenuous, they would have escorted me back, but I couldn't reach them.

Then we were moving, Mr Clegg and I, he forwards, me backwards. I was being edged towards the door till I was teetering on the edge of the step I had mounted just a moment ago. I tried one more time, my eyes pleading with this intractable man.

"Please, I can't *not* come out of the front door," I implored. I could have saved my breath. I was outside now, and I just couldn't fight anymore. I felt defeated.

Hating myself for my weakness, for my tremulous voice, I said, "I can't see the way." Tears were clouding my eyes. "Where do I go?" A derisive voice in my own head mocked me. *'Wimp,'* it spat. *'You sound like little-girl-lost; you can't even stand up for yourself.'*

"That way." Mr Clegg again waved an imperious arm in the general direction of a blank wall. Panic was taking over and I started to tremble, I couldn't see anything but a wall. My eyes pleaded again. "At the end, through the passage on the right," he barked at me, then went in and shut the white aluminium door.

I'd been dismissed. I felt like a servant girl who is no longer accepted at the big house, turned out into the world with just her meagre belongings. Terror gripped me as I stumbled along the wall that was supposed to lead to a passageway. *How could this be happening? What did I do to deserve this?*

Rain started to fall as drizzle, perfectly matching my emotions. *I must keep going, one foot in front of the other.* Like a weary marathon runner with the finishing line not yet in sight, I stumbled forward. I could see now that the wall was not attached to the building . . . the passageway! The narrow walkway led out to the main street and the front of the Old Bailey Courthouse. I had seen it from the front, but I'd always thought it was a dead end, just providing staff with side access. Reaching the end of the lane, I peered cautiously around the corner to my right, where I could see the waiting group of TV and print journalists, all in horseshoe formation, all waiting for me to emerge through the front door.

Dear God, I prayed, *what will they think when they see me walking from the alley? Will they think I was trying to get away from them? Will they run at me like they used to? Oh dear God, please help me, I feel so small and scared.* My heart was pounding in my chest, my palms were sweaty and I couldn't breathe properly.

Okay, okay, you can do this, Michelle, I told myself. *God gave you a vision. The hem of Christ's gown, remember? So as a follower of Christ, follow it. Keep your focus on his sandal. He is leading, walking ahead of you. You are safe!*

Taking a long restorative breath, I stepped out of the alleyway and into the street. No going back now. The 100 yard walk seemed interminable. Glancing up, I expected to see people and cameras rushing at me, but it appeared as though they would wait. Drawing nearer, I could hear the shuffling and jostling for position as microphones and cameras were readied.

Go on Michelle, one foot in front of the other. Follow Him, focus on Him.

As I arrived at the door, the waiting journalists tried to get me to look their way, to engage and start to speak, but I needed to regroup and calm myself. Instead of turning to face them, I turned right and escaped back inside the doorway, much to the further confusion of the waiting crowd. Tania and Surj came in with me and the door closed behind us, giving me some much needed privacy. By this time, I was close to hysterics. *What happened to our day of joy?*

Tania helped me to tidy myself, while Surj explained to the press that I'd be out in a moment. My mascara was smudged and I swiped at it with a fingertip hoping to remove the shadows caused by the rain and the tears. My hair was windblown and damp, but there was nothing much to be done about that now. Tania, satisfying herself that I would not collapse, took my hand and we headed back out to the waiting journalists and cameras. As I glanced around me, I caught sight of the oatmeal clad barrister across the street, exuding an air of bonhomie and hail-fellow-well-met as he laughed with two other men. Were they the security guards? They had all walked back through the building, but I wasn't allowed to do the same. I had been forced to walk around the outside in the rain.

Dragging my thoughts away from this blatant put-down, I turned to my waiting audience and, with a calmness I did not feel, started to speak.

"We are really delighted to finally have justice. We want to thank everybody who has supported us through all these years. Special thanks to Barry's legal team, to MOJO, and to all of the other agencies who help miscarriage of justice victims. A huge thank you to the jury; they obviously worked very hard to ensure they correctly interpreted the circumstantial evidence in this case.

"We've been fighting for many years. Now, we need time to get back together as a family. We also hope that the police will now look again into the murder of Jill Dando.

Thank you."

18

A Taste of Freedom

At last, I'd arrived at the hotel where Barry, Mike and Dr Young waited. I expected to find them celebrating and having fun, but Barry felt very exposed, and preferred not to have a fuss. He was terrified of anyone watching him, and felt other people would view revelry as in poor taste. This was not the celebration we had envisaged. We had thought we'd have a big party with all of the people who had helped in the campaign: MOJO, documentary makers, legal people, family and friends. We'd wanted to thank everyone for all they had done. Where had that gone? Why was this day so melancholic? We had fought so hard to get here.

I became aware that the unknown man and Barry were tête-à-tête with each other, and the man had a document Barry was intent on signing.

"What is that, Barry?"

"It's my contract for when I do interviews and stunt work, it will keep me safe?"

It seemed the man, David Wacks, was a solicitor. Barry had asked Jeremy for someone who could be his agent after he was freed, and Jeremy had brought in this man. Apparently, Barry had insisted I be kept out of this. He wanted to make his own decisions, and he was concerned that I would want to curb his enthusiasm for becoming a stuntman or doing other showbiz work.

"Barry, I'm very worried about you signing a contract. You've only just been released from prison." I asked him to wait a while but Barry was still determined, so I tried another avenue.

"Mr Wacks, maybe you can explain to me why Barry needs your services? What can you do for him? I'm not being awkward here, I'd just like to understand."

The answer did not allay my fears at all. He spoke of stunt work and film-extras work. He mentioned something about if a film were to be made about Barry's wrongful conviction, and that they would book him to make appearances. This didn't explain anything, so I tried again.

"Please, Mr Wacks, what will you do for Barry for 15% of any fee he receives? What protections can you offer him?"

It was my belief that Barry was too fragile to sign anything as important as this without discussion. This contract spanned a two year period. Barry was terrified of doing anything at all without legal protection and he thought this would provide that. However, the solicitor's response told me nothing, except that I should back off.

"Mr George knows what he wants and if you try to say he didn't, I'll bring people in who will testify that he knew full well what he was signing!"

Barry signed the contract, signing away a sizable chunk of the fee he would earn for his interviews with Sky and News of the World. This was the only money he would have to help him restart his life, because he was penniless and without possessions. It was Surj Singh Clair, working in his capacity as a MOJO volunteer, who had arranged this joint interview for Barry with Sky/NoW and had negotiated his fee. Surj wasn't seeking any remuneration from Barry. The contract Barry signed named both Mr Wacks and Jeremy Moore as his agents.

The reporters from News of the World suggested we all go up to the room reserved for Barry to do their interview. This wasn't a room, it was a huge suite! It had a super-king-sized bed, soft chairs, and loads of room for setting up for photographs. They had ascertained Barry's clothes sizes, because he was still wearing his prison garb. He was duly kitted out in black pants and a light blue shirt.

The interview commenced, and it went on for what seemed like forever, with only brief stops for comfort. Dr Young and I listened intently, correcting any errors we perceived. The finished text was read back to us and we all worked late into the night to finish and edit the article. At last, we could go to our own rooms for a much needed shower and some sleep.

The next morning, we all rose early. It was decided that we should have breakfast while it was quiet, since the hotel was so busy with bus tours. No such luck: the dining room was jammed with tourists clamouring to get their allotted meals before setting off on the next leg of their journey. Poor Barry ended up eating a rushed bite in his room while we scoffed down something indigestible downstairs, just to fill our empty bellies.

The News of the World and Sky News Corporation were trying hard to ensure that Barry wasn't recognised by too many people, because the hotel would then come under siege by other newspaper groups, who had been trying all sorts of tricks to find out where we were the night before. Apparently they had tried ringing all of the hotels in the area and asking for us, but we were not registered under our own names. Then they tried asking for Surj Singh Clair, but he was not registered here anymore. The News of the World had changed everything for the sake of anonymity. Protecting their 'exclusive' was paramount. It was important that we not speak to any other news group because of the exclusivity clause in the contract that Barry had signed with them. The last thing any of us needed was another media frenzy or being followed after we left the hotel.

In a family discussion the night before, as we sat bleary-eyed and exhausted, we agreed that we could not take Barry back to Mum's home because we would never be left alone by the overzealous journalists seeking to waylay us. We needed family time to reconnect with each other and plan how to move forward with our lives. Our expectation was that, after the story was published on Sunday, we'd have spoken enough through this interview and the one with Sky. We then hoped to be thought of as old news by everyone, and be left in peace.

One interview down, another to go. After our rushed food, which felt like lead in my stomach, it was time to take a dazed and bemused Barry into yet another room in the hotel. This time, it was the Sky News interview conducted by Kay Burley, an accomplished TV presenter with the Sky network. This was the interview I was dreading. I could reread and correct the words to be used by the newspaper, but this one would be broadcast for all the world to see and hear: it would be live. There would be no opportunity to edit or correct or explain if Barry constructed his sentences badly, which I had been able to with the newspaper journalists. This was a live broadcast. The world was watching.

No pressure then, I thought to myself ruefully, as we sat and waited for the crew to finish their preparations and count us down to 'on air'.

As the interview began, I became aware that I was grinning like a Cheshire cat. My nerves were jangling on high alert. Kay Burley was lovely towards Barry, even while asking the difficult questions about his previous convictions and his alibi for the day of the murder. Barry was very composed and coherent as I sat there with that ridiculous grin on my face, anticipating the need to wade in and rescue the situation, watching for any answer that could be ambiguous and therefore open to damaging Barry, rather than illustrating his innocence of the crime. Having Asperger's Syndrome, Barry's communication skills came under huge pressure, but he managed this cross-examination really well, only needing me to interject on his behalf a couple of times. It would have been hard not to feel proud of my brother as he maintained his composure through this very difficult situation. During the past few years, I'd had experience of many interview environments, but Barry had not worked with the media and had no previous experience to draw on. Yes, I was proud of this man, who had gone through so much, and come out the other side un-embittered.

The interview came to a close, and Kay got up to shake our hands and thank us for speaking with her. The room became a hive of activity again as the news crew checked various things and started to take apart the stage they had created earlier. My adrenalin levels were just settling back to normal when it happened: Barry innocently said something that sent ripples through the room. He asked Kay for her business card, and a look of anxiety crossed her face.

Poor Barry. He tried to explain that it was for his collection; a memory tactic he employed because of his short term memory loss and brain damage. He had no idea why she should react badly to his request. To him it was a normal, logical thing to do. It was also normal and logical for him to not take no for an answer, because he could not see the connections that we all saw standing out like a sore thumb. He just wanted the card because she had been the one to interview him. Of course, if anyone else had asked for it, they would probably have been given one with a smile, but this was Barry George, the man who had been convicted of killing a female TV presenter, even though he had been acquitted of the crime.

Oh my goodness, Barry, I thought, as I struggled to get him to see that this was being viewed as inappropriate behaviour. *Is this what it's going to be like from now on, lurching from one gaff to another, oblivious of the consequences?*

My adrenalin was now surging again, and I could feel the perspiration breaking out under my clothes from a mixture of fear and the heat of the lights in the makeshift studio. A male journalist with Sky came to the rescue, telling Barry that Kay had not brought cards with her today but that Barry could have one of his cards for his collection to remind himself of this momentous event.

Barry happily accepted this and placed the card into his pocket till we could buy him a wallet. Now, at last, we could leave and move on to our next hurdle: getting down to Portsmouth and to our family time together.

Having been let down by the justice system so many times, we hadn't put our faith in it to do the right thing this time. Therefore, I hadn't made any reservations for our retreat for after Barry's release. He might have been going back to prison to continue a life sentence for a crime he hadn't committed.

Of course, I had had discussions with Mum and with family and friends about what we might do if and when Barry was released, and so I had the bones of a plan ready for this welcome but fretful time. Thank God for good friends. My friend, Barry Loveday, a Reader in Criminal Justice at Portsmouth University, had given me some sage advice. Now it was time to implement it. Suddenly being faced with the reality of caring for the needs of this confused and frightened man, my mind was in turmoil, so there was no way I could have formulated any kind of plan. I felt utterly overwhelmed by the responsibility on my shoulders.

Dear Lord, when will this end? I just want some peace in my life . . . just an ordinary life!

Barry Loveday had suggested a hotel to me on the Isle of Wight. It was on the other side of the island, furthest away from the ferry ports, but that was not the only reason for the recommendation. He had felt that we would benefit from a little luxury, and also the peace and privacy this hotel complex could provide. It would be the perfect retreat for our little family to start getting to know each other again. Farringford had once been the home of poet laureate Alfred Lord Tennyson. It had the combined advantages of the sumptuous main house and the homey self-catering chalets. It also had an á la carte restaurant, and two separate ones in the grounds for the chalets: a fast food bar and a wine bar. It was perfect. This should provide a good choice to suit my pocket, since it was me who would have to fund it.

Thank you, Lord, for the life insurance pay-out; though I would not have sacrificed my husband's life for this. If I hadn't had this money, I don't know what we would have done.

So Farringford House on the Isle of Wight was the place I chose, where we would begin to reconnect with each other and to start the healing process we all so desperately needed. A country house retreat seemed the ideal location, far from the madding crowd.

We set off from the London hotel immediately after the Sky News interview. No lunch was offered, but the heavy-lying breakfast and the extreme mental strain meant we probably couldn't have eaten it anyway. When I told them I would be hiring a car to take us to our destination, the News of the World said they would provide us with a car and a driver. This wasn't an altruistic gesture on their part: their agenda was to keep us from being intercepted by rival journalists, thereby protecting their exclusive story until it broke on Sunday 10th August. They also arranged for hotel accommodation for us for one night, as part of this security.

It was known we were heading for Portsmouth, but I refused to give away our final destination, despite their probing and cajoling efforts to get the information from me. They wanted complete control over us, and I was not about to relinquish it to them. Agreeing to their offer of being chauffeur driven and of accommodation was to suit myself. I was really not confident of my ability to actually drive a long distance, such was my mental and physical agitation and stress. We had fulfilled our part of the bargain to be interviewed in order to be free of media constraints, and free we would be.

Being smuggled out of the hotel was melodramatic to say the least. We were taken to the elevator that serviced hotel guests, then down to the underground car park. The News of the World had even made sure lookouts were posted. They weren't very good, though, because at every floor someone got in or out with their luggage, which made me giggle at the absurdity of it all. Eventually, having reached the carpark without being outed, we were hustled to a waiting vehicle with smoky grey windows. We felt like foreign dissidents in a Bond movie, with all the dramatic subterfuge needed to rescue us from behind the Iron Curtain. We all found it very funny and didn't take it at all seriously, which did not please our protectors, as we were supposed to be very impressed indeed!

Our getaway car emerged from the darkened carpark and into the drizzly morning daylight without being followed or shot at – there were no photographers waiting outside. Our driver then navigated across London to Mum's home, all the while looking behind him for signs that we were being followed. He circled the block twice, just to be sure, then we pulled up outside of Mum's. Mum said she only had to check security, pick up the bags she'd left ready in the hall, and come back to the car; a few minutes at best. When she had been away quite a while I went to check on her, but she assured me all was well. She gave me one bag and said she would bring the rest. I'd been dismissed! So, placing her bag with mine in the boot of the car, I stood waiting for her to follow.

The car journey towards Portsmouth was the nearest we had come to relaxing since Barry was released on Friday. Mostly we sat in silence, watching the changing landscape go by, and allowing our bodies to come down from the state of high agitation we had been living under for the last 24 hours. It had been the culmination of 8 years of agitation and stress, really, and I wasn't sure I could ever fully come down from it. We all felt mentally and physically exhausted; our adrenaline levels were depleted. We were headed to a hotel in Portsmouth, funded by the News of the World, just for one night. Then we would be on our own.

About halfway in our journey, Mum emerged from her silence and quietly announced, "I think I left my handbag at home with my medication in it."

My fraught mind and body wanted to shoot back up to high anxiety again, but I took a deep breath and tried to bring the panic under control. *Is anything going to go right?*

"Oh, Mum, we can't go back for it now. Don't worry, we'll find a doctor and have a prescription emailed through. We'll cope without the bag."

"I'll be alright," came Mum's tired reply. "They're not that important, we don't have to bother the doctor." Poor Mum. She seemed so exhausted, and she was trying not to add to the stress. I settled back down to my landscapes and reverie. Little did I know, *this* was the calm before the storm!

A mobile phone, chirruping, broke the silence in the car and brought me back to reality. It was our driver's phone, and he spoke to the caller for a couple of moments; he seemed to be confused about something. He then proceeded to relay some of the call to me.

I was flabbergasted! A three-way discussion then ensued between the caller, the driver, and me, until he couldn't deal with the call any longer, and passed the phone over to me in the back of the cab to communicate directly.

The News of the World were refusing to pay Barry his fee for the interview! *Why?* We had all worked so hard on this once-and-for-all piece. I couldn't get my head around what was happening. Apparently the driver had been told to get us to Portsmouth, then just to drop us wherever we wanted to go, because they were finished with us. What we did or where we went was up to us, they didn't care.

My heart was pumping furiously, and my head was filled with that whirring, buzzing sound that often precedes fainting. I took the handset, and once again went in to battle for Barry, and against injustice. *How? Why would they do this to him, to us?*

"What's happening here, what's the problem?" I tried to sound calm and unruffled, even though I again felt that the world was spinning out of control. I had to be able to get this sorted out. It was inconceivable that Barry should lose his fee. What would he use to set up his life again if he didn't have this? All he owned had been taken from him when the police took him into custody for a crime he didn't commit. He had nothing in the world but the plastic bag he had brought to court, which contained a change of clothes. He needed this money to feed and clothe himself in the coming months, to buy the essentials to live, to pay rent. I couldn't fund all of this!

Maybe this was all a misunderstanding and could be sorted in a couple of minutes. *Stay calm, Michelle, it can't possibly be as bad as it seems ... just check out what they're saying and correct them. Legally they have to pay, otherwise they are breaking the contract. Take a deep breath ...*

"Barry has broken the contract he signed with us and has given an exclusive interview to the Sunday Mirror," the voice informed. "Therefore, we are not paying him the fee. The driver will leave you in Portsmouth, we're not involved with you anymore." This was announced in a peremptory tone by the caller from the News of the World. Then silence, as they waited for my response.

"Don't be ridiculous, of course he hasn't. How could he have done that? He hasn't been out of your sight!"

"The Sunday Mirror have announced they have the exclusive, so he must have spoken to them," came the cold, unemotional response.

"What?! You know that's not true, you kept him under wraps yourselves. He hasn't spoken with anyone since signing your contract, none of us have. You made sure that no one got near him. This is utterly ridiculous. They have to be lying. Barry has kept his bargain with you, you have to pay him. If you don't, you have to pull the story; we will withdraw our consent." I thought they were pulling a fast one on us.

"The journalist for the Sunday Mirror is a Scott Lomax, do you know him?"

Scott Lomax? Of course I knew him. He was the man who had worked with Mike on the 'Justice For Barry' website for years. He had written two books about the case: *Who Killed Jill Dando?: The Case of Barry George, A Shocking Miscarriage of Justice* and *The Case Of Barry George*. These both showed all the flaws in the evidence. Barry had spoken with him briefly after Scott rang Mike on his mobile, and Scott had asked if he could congratulate Barry, just after we'd arrived at the hotel. Barry, of course, was anxious to thank Scott for all the work he'd done for him. Scott wouldn't pull a stunt like this, why would he? There had to be another explanation. I told the voice on the phone as much.

"There's no mistake, and it doesn't matter to us. It's a breach of contract, and we're not paying. The story will not be pulled, either. We're running it."

The line went dead.

What now? What do I do? This had to be a huge, ghastly mistake. I know, I'll ring Surj, he'll know what to do. I relayed the story.

"I'll get on to them and sort this out, Michelle, you just relax. I'll ring you back in a while."

This went on, back and forth, until we reached Portsmouth. It had been agreed that the News of the World would still put us up at the hotel, and would review the whole situation overnight, but the story would still run. Surj suggested I put everything aside, try to unwind, and get some sleep. *The chances of that are slim to none,* I thought, but sleep I did. I was so exhausted, but I rose refreshed and ready for a new battle. Oh, the restorative power of sleep, and an unshakable faith in God that He would resolve this new injustice.

The following morning was Barry's first day of almost unfettered freedom. We met in the hotel's breakfast room where, because of his recent incarceration, Barry was totally overawed by the huge buffet on offer. He had no idea what he could have, I had to take him around and guide him.

In prison, normal social skills are lost and need to be relearned. A released felon is given training to do this while still on the inside, but a wrongly convicted person is just put out and must fend for themselves. There is no help with making a return to society.

I picked up a small breakfast for Mum, too. She wouldn't have eaten anything otherwise, she was feeling so overwhelmed. As we sat trying to eat our meal, a man approached us.

"Are you Barry George?"

Barry looked askance at me.

"Yes, he is," I answered warily. "Can we help you?" We didn't know what this man wanted. Did he want to thump Barry or congratulate him? It was a tense moment as we waited for a response.

"Well done, you! I am so pleased to actually meet you! Never thought you were guilty, and now you're free." With that, he took Barry's hand and began to pump it up and down, enthusiastically. "Can I take a photo with you to show my friends?" He was lining himself up for a selfie on his smartphone.

Here I had to draw the line.

"I'm sorry, we can't, but thank you for your kindness and for stopping by." There was no way I was going to add fuel to the fire by breaching the photos clause in the News of the World contract. Anyway, this guy could well have been one of their journalists checking up on us.

Am I becoming paranoiac on top of everything else? I thought. It was hard not to be, after everything.

The man went on his way, and we returned to our breakfasts. There was an important visit to make later this morning before going over to the Isle of Wight. We'd been invited to the home of Sion and Tina Jenkins. Barry was meeting with Sion, another wrongly convicted man, for the first time. I'd made friends with Sion and Tina and had stayed with them in the past, having met Sion at the MOJO conference in Glasgow where I was a guest speaker. He and Tina lived in a lovely Victorian terraced home in Portsmouth. The entranceway was overgrown with tall shrubs and old-fashioned flowers. Seeing these two sorely victimised men, arms wrapped about each other and talking with heads together, excluding us women as only people who have shared an experience might do, it made my heart swell with joy. I offered up thanks to God for both of their lives. Tina had gone off to her period-style kitchen to make hot drinks all round. I glanced at Mum, and it was easy to see that she, too, was a bit overcome by this auspicious meeting.

We finished our tea and coffee and settled down to some conversation while we waited for Barry Loveday to arrive, then we were all off to the local Indian restaurant for a celebratory lunch. It was a great choice by Sion, since Barry and I shared a love of Indian cuisine. I enjoyed the wonderful flavours and aromatic spices, the burst of perfume in my mouth when I bit into a cardamom pod, and Barry loved a burning hot curry just like Dad.

We'd walked from the house to the restaurant, pleased by the fact there were no photographers to be seen. What a relief that was to us all, but especially to these two persecuted men who walked side by side, determined to reclaim their right to freedom. We all walked behind them, like Noah's animals, two by two.

The restaurant was good, the food was delightful, and the conversation flowed like the lively rosé wine I had chosen to accompany the meal. It was a near normal experience for people living anything but normal lives, and a very welcome respite for me as the carer. I was sorry when it ended and we had to go on our way again.

My next challenge was to book the chalet at Farringford. I could hardly book it in the name of 'George'. Neither could I use my name, Diskin, as that would be recognisable also, and I didn't want to say who we were in case someone alerted the press that we were there. My heart was in my mouth as I rang and booked us in under an assumed name.

Getting from one side of the island to the other was another challenge. Public transport would take hours and would leave a much easier trail to follow for the media. Besides, we were all too tired for that. I decided to use some of my limited resources and pay for a taxi to drive us there. The News of the World, via their driver, had assertively offered the use of their driver for wherever we were going, but I had insisted on leaving him in Portsmouth, much to their annoyance. It wouldn't take long for them to pick up the scent again, and I wanted us to have arrived at our destination before then. All this subterfuge didn't come easily. It seemed to require so much mental dexterity, and mine was quickly running out. Some acting skills and having very few scruples would have been an asset, too: lying to people pricked at my conscience like needles.

Our chalet at Farringford was a two-bedroomed, 1940s style cottage with a sparsely-equipped kitchen. It was painted green and cream throughout to match the décor of the period. To us it was a refuge, a cushion from the outside world where we felt like hunted animals. Here, we could hole up and lick our wounds. My laptop and dongle was to prove invaluable, Barry needed his *wants* met immediately, and I was brain dead. I used the computer to set him tasks he needed to learn, or let him do research that he wanted to do, then left him to work while I mentally tuned out. Being a round-the-clock carer felt akin to being an army leader guiding his war-weary and battered troops to safety. I was certainly not equipped for it.

On Sunday, the News of the World ran the story and it was a hatchet job. Barry's piece was fine, except for the headline . . .

'I couldn't have done it, I was stalking another woman at the time!' Barry absolutely *did not* say this. We'd been there the entire time, we'd gone over everything. Barry told them, "I couldn't have killed Jill Dando. I was talking with another woman at the time."

Actually, he was wrong. When Ms Dando was killed, Barry was at the HAFAD centre. Barry doesn't have a concept of time, that's why he often runs into difficulties. Added to that, all of Barry's teeth are missing so he speaks with a slight lisp. The News of the World took 'was-talking' and made it 'was-stalking', but we hadn't noticed. To this day people still think he said this, and make judgements about him based on it, but he didn't.

This publication also carried two other articles on the Jill Dando/ Barry George story, making a spread over three pages. Both of these were horrendous. Never have I seen such vitriol aimed at someone who has been found not guilty. Retired Detective Ian Horrocks, one of the original officers on the case, had a whole section devoted entirely to saying that the police did not make a mistake, and many other things that made Barry look guilty. We were dumbstruck by all of this. To my knowledge, it was unprecedented to attack a person in this way when they've been exonerated. If the police had had any more evidence against Barry, they would have used it. There was none, therefore he was freed. What would be the gain in keeping Barry incarcerated, with Jill's killer still walking freely among us?

From here on, it was open season on Barry George in the press. We were sought out and photographed from afar, untrue stories were emblazoned on front pages with lurid headlines. Many times he was with people who could vouch for him, but no one cared. They were vilifying him, and that would sell papers. We were naïve to think that one article, or even a not guilty verdict, would mean we would ever be left alone.

Back on the Isle of Wight, we were still battling to get the newspaper to pay Barry for his exclusive interview. Barry's new solicitor, Mr Wacks, wanted him to take a lesser amount. He had spoken with the paper's representatives and they said they would pay a sixth of the fee, or a bit more if Barry would submit to a lie detector test. I was utterly outraged that his solicitor would even think this was acceptable! Not guilty, by a unanimous jury verdict, is not guilty. Barry had nothing to prove, and in his mental state he could not have coped with that kind of stress. I turned it down flat, but later ran the idea by Dr Young, who emphatically agreed with me. The stress on Barry was already immense; he should not be put through this, too.

Meanwhile, Mum was growing quieter. I thought it was her reaction to all the stress, but eventually she told me she needed her medication. She was feeling very ill. Now we *had* to visit a local doctor to try to get a prescription for her. This took a whole day, but we were grateful for all who played their part in getting help for Mum. Thank you to the relative who contacted the family GP, and to those at the medical facility in Freshwater. Brookside Health Centre liaised with Mum's GP and gave an emergency prescription of the medication she needed.

Whilst on the Isle of Wight, Barry had become very depressed because I would not let him out of my sight. My virtual house arrest seemed so unfair, but I felt certain it was the right move for his safety. One night we went for a long walk around the golf course, picking our way in the inky darkness. He poured out his heart to me, crying and saying he felt like he was still inside. Much as this hurt, I did not relent, and this was to prove vital for Barry a few weeks later.

We stayed on the island for thirteen days in all, travelling back by train to London. The News of the World had relented and decided they would pay Barry his full fee, thanks to the Trojan efforts of Surj Singh Clair. Barry's own solicitor had been unable to do anything to help Barry, though he still received his fifteen percent. Surj, of course, did not earn a penny from Barry for his efforts, because he was representing MOJO and not himself.

19

Escape from Persecution

"Barry George, the loner cleared of the murder of Jill Dando, will be interviewed by Hampshire Police about the attempted rape of a teenage girl."

The Telegraph and other papers carried this salacious headline and accompanying article on the 5th October 2008. It went on to say that Barry George had harassed a woman in London and had been thrown out of Sky Studios when he'd cycled there looking for Kay Burley, claiming that he wanted a copy of a television interview she did with him upon his release. He was removed from the premises.

Back in Cork, I was distraught. Surj had already contacted the Sky Studios' security department. They'd confirmed Barry did come on his bicycle, but that he was well-mannered and had *not* been thrown out, rather he was happy that Sky would post out a copy of his interview to him. He did not ask for Kay Burley, either. Why would fellow journalists make up scare stories like this? Kay must have been terrified. She was already under stress over an alleged assault on a photographer, and this could have pushed her over the edge. It seemed they would sacrifice anything and anyone in order to turn a quick buck. A pack mentality.

"Hello Michelle, I'm sorry to disturb you." I recognised the voice of Nick Baird, Barry's solicitor, since he'd changed firms again after his release. Nick speaks with a slightly bored drawl, and has a wickedly dry sense of humour. It was always good to run things by

Nick, and we got along very well, despite not always understanding each other's humour. We'd had many conversations about the newspaper articles that were appearing with alarming regularity.

"I've just had a phone call from Hampshire Police, Michelle. They wanted permission from me to speak with Barry about that attack on the Isle of Wight." Nick sounded almost animated, which was unusual for him . . . this was not good. "I asked them if my client was a suspect, and they said no, so I told them they were not to go to my client's home to interview him. I phoned Barry to let him know they'd spoken to me. Shortly after, Barry rang me to say three plain-clothed detectives came to his apartment and tried to prevent him from leaving, asking to go inside for a chat. Barry was just leaving because of my call, so he pushed past them into the street. He wouldn't go into the apartment with them as he was afraid of what they might do. Apparently, after Barry left, the detectives went to your mother's house looking for him, but he'd had more sense, he'd gone to his MJSS case worker, Carla. Michelle. I am very worried for him. Is there anything you can do?"

Oh, no. Here we go again.

"Nick, I'll ring Mum and Barry and see what I can find out, then I'll get back to you." A plan was forming in my mind.

"Hi Mum, I hear you had visitors today?" I quipped.

"Oh yes I did! Them b****y detectives!" She almost spat the words. "Came to *my door* asking for Barry. He doesn't live here! I told them, but they wanted to come in and check for themselves, look around his bedroom, if you please. Cheeky so and so's." *Boy she was mad!*

"What do they want him for, anyway? He's an innocent man, he didn't kill no one, why can't they just leave him alone? I wouldn't let them in, no telling what they'd do in my home. Then they changed tactics . . . 'Maybe you can help us, Mrs George, we like to know what you saw on the Isle of Wight when you were there with Barry and your daughter.'

"What did I see? What did I see?! *Scenery*, that's what I saw. And if you want any more information, you can contact my daughter. She did all the driving."

Well done Mum! I'm still waiting to be interviewed by Hampshire Police.

A little while later I did some research into the attack on this poor sixteen-year-old girl in Freshwater. The attacker was described as wearing dark clothes, and having dark hair, probably about 5' 10" in height . . . and skinny! After eight years in a prison, Barry was obese. Not exactly something one can disguise. Where was the compassion for this young victim? The police and the media used her ordeal to, again, emblazon Barry's name in the papers, to portray him to the public as a monster.

Okay, what's next? I thought as I tried to pull this plan together. *Oh yes, phone Carla. After that, Hazel, then back to Carla, then Mum, then Nick, then Barry . . .* It was going to be a long day. No wonder I felt dizzy half the time.

"Barry, you have to get away," I warned him later on. "I know you didn't want me to interfere, but this is no longer something you can handle alone, this is a witch hunt." Actually, he had not been handling anything, but Barry had refused to accept my help so I'd had to step back. I'd even had members of the press remonstrating with me for not protecting him, then writing trash, but I couldn't help him if he wouldn't let me. Now we were past that: he was extremely vulnerable, and could not even go back to his apartment to collect his medication or belongings. More lost items he'd never be compensated for.

The consensus after all the phone calls had been to get him to safety, urgently.

My flight into Leeds Bradford International Airport had been booked for weeks, because I was to attend a conference run by United Against Injustice, where Sion Jenkins was to be a guest speaker. On this occasion I was just a delegate; it had been nice not to have to write a speech or stand at the front delivering one. I was going there to support Sion, because these conferences are always so difficult. I also hoped my presence might encourage others who still had loved ones wrongfully imprisoned that they, too, would someday see justice. This arrangement was quickly changed when Sion was taken ill at home and couldn't make it. On the day, and with no preparation, I was asked to step in and speak.

My plan had been to fly into Leeds, stay at a local hotel for a couple of nights, then fly back home to Cork. Now all these plans would have to change; a lot of money paid out for fares would be lost, and more would be spent besides. It was arranged that Barry would travel from London to Birmingham, where he would be met by volunteers from MOJO. They would take him to a secret location and keep him safe. In two days, he and a volunteer, Russ, would meet me in Leeds. When Russ returned to his family, Surj would take over, taking Barry along to a meeting he was having at another hotel.

We really hoped that all of these precautions would mean Barry would not appear in any more disgraceful headlines, but no. They were being followed everywhere, even camping outside of Russ' home looking for Barry, though they were not there. Russ' wife and family felt intimidated by the media's presence. The only way they could have known about Russ was if our phones were being monitored. Of course, this was all before the Leveson Inquiry and the News of the World's well-earned downfall.

Story upon story was published. There was one story that alleged Barry had terrified a nurse in the hospital carpark, and that he was in an agitated state demanding drugs at the hospital. The truth was that he was with Russ and they had gone to A&E to replace Barry's epilepsy meds, as he'd had to abandon his supply at the flat when the police came. Another story alleged that he was now obsessed with Cheryl Cole as well as Kay Burley, and that he was dating a convict's wife, the person Surj went to a business meeting with!

Coming down for a snack in the hotel that evening, Barry and I saw journalists casually draped across couches and easy chairs together, having drinks and a great laugh at our expense. They didn't try to hide who they were, they didn't care that Barry could prove these stories were lies. They would write whatever they wanted, whenever they wanted, and were perfectly happy to make it all up. Apparently, nothing else newsworthy was happening in the world: no earthquakes or famines, no wars, all was at peace. Anyway, what could Barry George do to them? They were the untouchables!

Sleep would not come that night. I spent the time formulating an escape strategy. It all sounds so exaggerated now, but it was real and very scary. I spoke with Paddy Hill, who gave some advice, then no more phone calls. We were on our own. I would not risk another overheard conversation.

We rose early the next morning, hopefully before the hunters had finished sleeping off their refreshments from the night before. No taxis; we walked to the bus station, dragging our luggage. I had booked tickets on a National Express bus to Cairnryan in Scotland. We were going to Cork, via Belfast. Never have I prayed so hard in my entire life.

God, please, please, don't let them work out what we are doing. Lord, you need to go before us, you know what we need. Please, let us reach Scotland before they have time to work out our plans. Knowing the arrogance of those stalking us, they would probably assume they could pick up the scent again in London. Where else would we go?

Our journey to Cork took twenty-four hours from Leeds through to Ballincollig. It was a nerve-wracking marathon expedition. It's just an hour's plane trip away, but I couldn't take Barry by plane because he had no passport. It was amongst the belongings taken from his apartment in 2000, and now the police said they didn't have it. Travel within the UK didn't require one, which was why we opted for the route via Belfast. Belfast is part of the UK. It is also on the island of Ireland, so it gave us a way for Barry to cross into the South without a passport.

So fraught was this journey that, on a scheduled rest stop at a motorway services, I was bursting for the toilet facilities. My stress levels were sky high, my blood-pressure was probably even higher and everything was blurred. Locating the loos, I rushed headlong in, dived into a cubicle and . . . looking around me, the realisation dawned that something was very wrong. I was in the gents! Going in had not been too bad, but coming out was a little more difficult, as it had now filled up with fellow facility-seekers of the male variety. Oops.

Belfast to Dublin, Dublin to Cork, Cork to Ballincollig. We were like wet dishrags when we arrived; we hadn't slept for two nights, and now I had to sleep in my sitting room to give Barry my bedroom. Despite it all, though, we had done it. Barry had been rescued from the country of his birth, and taken to one that knew miscarriages of British justice intimately.

Barry was entitled to an Irish passport because Mum was Irish by birth, so we applied, receiving it quickly, much to Barry's dismay. He was certain that his name alone would ensure he was turned down. Then he was worried the media would highlight that he had an Irish passport and the police would take it away. Every long-serving miscarriage of justice victim I had met had been forced to reapply for their British passport because the police said they didn't have them. Victimised, and suffering PTSD, they would have to explain to unsympathetic civil servants that they had been wrongly incarcerated for years and that's why their passport was lost. This heaped humiliation, like salt, into their open wounds.

Barry so wanted to start his free life, but he felt he'd never be allowed to. He was afraid that if he returned to Britain, the police would pick him up on trumped-up charges and he would disappear without a trace. He was seriously worried for his safety, and his disabilities only added to this problem.

On one such trip back to London, he was meeting up with his friend and QC Ian Glen at a central London coffee shop, when he was stopped and searched for no reason. Ian witnessed the officers stopping Barry, although he wasn't doing anything, and wasn't behaving in a worrying or threatening way. They left when Barry pointed Ian out to them.

If Barry had been a dangerous offender recently released, I would have been right behind this monitoring of his movements by the police. Indeed, I would have never fought for his freedom from the sentence in the first place. If you do the crime, you must do the time. I'd have expected him to serve out his full sentence. However, Barry was not a released offender, he hadn't killed anyone. He was a wrongly convicted man, and his previous convictions from the eighties were now spent and had been since 1992. No matter how appalled I was at those crimes, they were long in the past, 26 years ago, and he was not a registered sex offender. Why, then, was he being harassed in the street? We believe it was the conviction for the murder of Jill Dando.

Barry had been put under a Multi-Agency Public Protection Arrangement order, or a MAPPA order, whilst still in prison. Having been found not guilty at retrial, we felt that this order should have been rescinded, since he was not under any such order before this wrongful conviction. MAPPA orders are measures put in place to protect the public from harm when sexual or violent offenders are freed. The person is monitored by the police, prison and probation services, as well as other agencies, such as local housing authorities, youth offending teams, health trusts, social services, and job centres. In 2008, the criteria covered were registered sexual offenders, violent offenders or other dangerous offenders. According to Barry's mental health team, he did not fit any of these criterion. His MJSS officer also said he did not belong in any of these categories. If he was not required to be under such an order before his wrongful conviction, why was he under one after said conviction had been quashed?

The Met Police said this had nothing to do with his conviction in 2001. They had carried out a risk assessment, using a mathematical equation constructed on age and convictions (but his convictions were spent!) and based on this they had come up with him possibly reoffending (after 26 years?). He had not needed this order before Jill Dando had been killed. Barry took a case against this decision but lost, having to pay the costs himself.

Being under this MAPPA order has seriously affected Barry's ability to access help for his PTSD. He would not attend anywhere for counselling because he was convinced they would have to tell the police everything he said, and he was afraid of the police, with good reason. Actually, he was right: they could have been compelled to report everything. Mum and I could have been in serious trouble, too, if we had not given the police all information pertaining to his movements when asked. It is right that released offenders who fall into these categories of violence are put under such an order; this is an important safeguard for the public. However, someone wrongly convicted should not. It is intimidation.

Most victims of miscarriage of justice will need help with post-traumatic stress, but most will never get it, because the government won't fund it. Paddy Hill and MOJO have offered to help these people, and also returning military personnel with PTSD, by opening a centre for them where they can be given counselling and be taught everyday life skills again. Certain skills are lost in destructive circumstances like wrongful convictions and warfare conditions.

MOJO desperately need funding for this project, but again the government have said no. Sir Terry Waite, CBE, humanitarian and former hostage in Beirut, spoke at the MOJO conference on PTSD in Glasgow in 2007. He talked of his inability to interact with other people after his return, even family members. He recounted the painfully judgemental brush with the media who had no inkling of his psychological damage; they just wanted the fanfare and hurrahs. Terry's needs were secondary to theirs. He spoke of how he only recovered as well as he did because of the specialist help given by RAF medical personnel on his return. They allowed him to eat alone, because he could not eat with other people due to his enforced isolation in captivity. He could have short visits from loved ones until he was strong enough to deal with extended company and conversation. Offenders on phased release get help to relearn social skills. Quite the reverse happens to the wrongly convicted, the factually innocent. They are put out of the prison, then left to their own devices. Sink or swim.

Paddy Hill writes in his book, *Forever Lost; Forever Gone:*
"I just wanted a packet of fags and a tube of toothpaste."

Paddy insisted on going to the shop for these himself after his release in 1991, but he had never encountered a six-lane highway before and nearly lost his life crossing it. Then he asked the shop assistant for his items, only to be directed 'down that aisle'. Paddy only remembered shops where the shop staff served you from behind the counter. Supermarkets and self-service checkouts were unheard of and were entirely alien to him.

The changes that have taken place in the world – technology, the cost of living, value of currency – all need to be relearned by someone who has been incarcerated for a protracted period. Terry Waite recognised this and that was why he spoke at the same meeting I did, for MOJO. Terry is an inspirational man; I feel honoured to have met him.

20

Not Innocent Enough

*'Barry George in line for £500,000 compensation for his
eight-year ordeal behind bars.'*

The world was informed by headlines such as this that Barry was to
make a fortune from compensation for this wrongful conviction.
Of course they, and his legal team, knew this was not so. £500,000
is the absolute ceiling that can be awarded to the wrongly convicted,
but it's rarely given to anyone. Barry could never hope to qualify
for that figure, not with only eight years in prison and with no loss
of a career.

Barry's legal team duly applied for compensation, however little
it might be. He was turned down because, they were told, Barry
was not a miscarriage of justice. There had been evidence against
him, and the Crown Prosecution Service was not wrong to take
the case. The fact that there was no evidence linking Barry to Jill's
murder, nor was there a motive for him to have carried out this
crime, plus the fact that he had been found 'not guilty' at retrial by
a unanimous verdict seemed not to matter. Technically, the law says
he is not a miscarriage of justice because "a jury, properly directed,
could have found him guilty" (Section 133, Criminal Justice Act).

This amendment has meant that most people released after
appeal will not receive a penny. At the time of writing this book,
there are legal cases lining up to show that this change to the system
is unlawful, unworkable and unjust.

The presumption of innocence is enshrined in the British justice system. A defendant is not required to prove their innocence because it is for the prosecution to prove guilt. Should the trial break down, the presumption of innocence is carried forward to the new trial, as it was in Barry's case in 2001 due to the media scandal.

Barry has been severely disadvantaged by not being informed of this need to prove his innocence before his re-trial. A court of law is the only forum where this could have been done. Because this law was put in place and is retrospectively applied, no effort was put into proving Barry's innocence: it wasn't necessary. No extra funding was made available to the defence team; the funding was for the prosecution and the onus was with them to prove guilt. The legal team, and Barry, believed that 'not guilty' meant there was nothing left standing against him. Our justice system has moved the goal posts mid-game.

When Barry's appeal against the 2001 conviction was upheld in 2007, I thought the new trial would start with this presumption: Barry would be considered innocent unless the jury found him guilty. I believed the quashed conviction meant the same as there being no conviction standing against him. After all, it had been overturned. Alison Saunders of the Crown Prosecution Service and the trial Judge had both said, "Mr George now has the right to be regarded as an innocent man."

However, it seems Barry is still considered partially guilty by those who award compensation. Even though there is no mechanism for this within our justice system, it seems that an acquitted person must now prove their own innocence 'beyond reasonable doubt'. Not guilty, or acquitted, now means half innocent, almost there. In England we do not have a finding in our courts of 'not proven'; one is either guilty or innocent. Barry had been assured that a retrial would prove, once and for all, that there was no evidence capable of implicating him in the case against him. Now *that* had been turned on its head. Ian Glen QC (now sadly deceased), representing Barry in his claim for compensation, was incensed. Just how innocent is innocent? He coined the phrase 'Not Innocent Enough'!

Under international law, the UK has an obligation to compensate victims of wrongful conviction. Until 2006, we had two systems in place to help with redress: The Statutory Scheme and the Ex-Gratia Scheme. The Ex-Gratia Scheme would have helped people like Barry, who didn't qualify as a miscarriage of justice. They could still have been given a discretionary sum by the Home Secretary to help them start to rebuild their lives. However, Tony Blair's government, and then Home Secretary Charles Clarke, removed the discretionary scheme, leaving released non-offenders to restart life with £47 given to them when they were released from prison. Today, the government and judiciary are refusing compensation in most cases, using this get-out clause.

Far from improving after the exoneration of the Guildford Four, the Birmingham Six and the Maguire Seven, the justice system seems to have become even more unjust. I see an arrogance by those in government, and by high ranking judiciary, towards the lives of those they are supposed to serve. In 1990, Lord Denning famously said if the Guildford Four had been hanged, "They'd probably have hanged the right men. Not proved against them, that's all."

He also said: "Hanging ought to be retained for murder most foul: We wouldn't have all these campaigns to get the Birmingham Six released if they'd been hanged. They'd have been forgotten, and the whole community would be satisfied . . . It is better that some innocent men remain in jail than that the integrity of the English judicial system be impugned."

This still seems to be the thinking of many in government and the judiciary today.

The criminal justice system is where we as citizens can go to get redress or retribution when we believe we have been wronged. Whatever the crime, we expect the system to give us justice, to accept the righteousness of our cause and to put it right. The guilty must be caught and called to account, then punished for their wrongdoings. Society needs such a system if it is not to descend into anarchy and vigilante or mob rule.

However, we must remember, the system is not some computer programme that has gone haywire. It is a living, breathing organisation, run by real flesh and blood people, people who must stop abdicating responsibility and take steps to resolve the wrongs endemic in it. Many who work within the justice system are only too well aware of the flaws; they encounter them all the time. Those heroic people, far too many to mention here, work tirelessly and often pro bono to put right the wrongs.

Guilt or innocence is not at the heart of the British Justice System. It is only concerned with whether due process can be seen to have been followed. The system needs to be reformed, but it will not look at its wrongs in order to correct them, and until it does there will be more wrongful convictions. The taxpayer will have to keep on footing the bill for people to be unfairly incarcerated in our prisons, leaving the guilty free to offend again.

Barry can prove his innocence. The retrial showed that he was at the HAFFAD centre at a time that made it impossible for him to have committed the crime. The trial judge, in his summing up to the jury, said: "If you believe that Mr George was at the disability centre between 11.40 and 12 o'clock, then he could not have committed the crime, and you must acquit."

How much more proof of innocence does Barry need?

Britain wants the world to believe it has the best justice system, indeed, that it is the envy of the world. Conversely, it does not live up to this high standard. It ought to be striving to achieve this prominent position, not hiding its abuses away in a prison cell. There are certainly enough countries in the world with appalling human rights abuses – just a glimpse of the news shows that this world is in turmoil. Britain could, and should, lead the way in implementing reforms, starting with its own injustices. Reform of the justice system needs to start with changing attitudes.

Jesus said:

> "You hypocrite, first take the plank out of your own eye, and then you will see clearly to remove the speck from your brother's eye."
> (Matthew 7:5 NIV)

21

Losing Mum

Mum only ever gave one interview to the press on her own. In her interview with the Daily Mirror, Mum expressed her concern about not living long enough to see her son freed. Thankfully, Mum did live to see her son released. She also lived long enough to see his fight back from the horrific, discriminatory maltreatment meted out by an out of control media circus. Being able to stay with Barry at his apartment when she visited Ireland brought a measure of closure for her. She loved Ballincollig, and she loved attending our church with us. She and I had many discussions about salvation and Heaven over the years as we walked and talked on our days out in interesting places like Bandon, Blarney, Youghal and Cobh, all in County Cork.

"You know, Mum, it's comforting for us to know that we'll meet Pat again when we get to Heaven."

For a long time, Pat couldn't understand what had happened to his family, and why he felt on the outside. He came to church, heard the same Bible verses he'd heard over and over, but just didn't quite understand. Now I was opening up a subject that I felt Mum had not fully appreciated, either, when we'd talked of God and salvation. Since we were visiting the different churches in Bandon, the topic seemed ripe for discussion.

On one of my many trips to London, my daughter Carine had gone to her Dad and asked, "Dad, will you watch this video for me, please?"

It was part one of the Left Behind series by Tim LaHaye and Jerry B Jenkins, two US Christian authors. The series is a work of fiction based around the book of Revelation in the Bible. She handed the video cassette to him.

"Of course I will, darling, but why?"

"Because I don't want you to be left behind, Dad."

She had been so concerned that whenever he might die, he would not go to Heaven, but be separated from God. Each of the children had accepted Jesus as their saviour and knew they would be with Him in Heaven someday.

To say Pat had a 'lightbulb experience' is to understate it. In a flash, he understood that he had never made a commitment to God, and *that* was what was making him feel like we all shared something he was not a part of. He recalled hearing the verses in Romans 10:9-10: *'If you declare with your mouth, "Jesus is Lord," and believe in your heart that God raised him from the dead, you will be saved. For it is with your heart that you believe and are justified, and it is with your mouth that you profess your faith and are saved.'*

I wasn't there to witness this interaction between father and daughter, but Pat told me himself later that night when he phoned to share his news. He wanted to declare with his mouth to me first, then he was going to see our preacher, Ernie Tromsness.

I was stunned. Pat was crying. Ernie was jubilant. This was amazing news. Our little family would always be that much closer now. Carine later told me it had taken a lot of courage to challenge her Dad on this issue, and that she'd been sure he'd brush her aside. Funnily enough, he never did watch the video, but now he didn't need to.

Mum had her questions, too.

"Don't we all go to Heaven?" This question was thrown out as a challenge, and delivered in a snappy tone. I was unsure how to explain, but I knew I had to try.

"Mum, your Bible says the same as mine: salvation is through Jesus. We are to repent of our sins, which means be truly sorry for them, before he will forgive us. Why would He allow the unrepentant into Heaven? Does the God you know tell you lies?"

Many more discussions were to follow, but for now Mum was thinking about things, and not just accepting what she thought she'd been taught, just like Pat.

Mum died unexpectedly on Monday 5th September 2011, whilst in Ireland on holiday. We had been to church on Sunday, then travelled to visit more family in Limerick. She suffered a catastrophic stroke and was gone. It left us shattered and numbed, but in all of our conversations about dying, Mum had always said, "When my time comes, I don't want to know about it."

She hadn't known. What was a painful event for us was a blessing for Mum, and we took solace in that.

Barry missed his Mum terribly. He struggled to articulate his emotions, but it was plain to see in the lost expression in his hazel-brown eyes. He also missed the home we had been brought up in. Mum hadn't owned her home, and so it reverted back to the housing authority after she died. I missed my Mum, too. There's a Mum-shaped place in my heart that only she could fill. I miss our trips to the coffee shop, Mum outraged at the prices but rarely turning down a great coffee and walnut cake. I miss phoning Mum and hearing, 'What's the weather like?' It was very painful clearing the house, sending pre-loved possessions to the charity shops and homeless organisations, but Mum would have approved.

Locking the front door for the last time, misty thoughts of the first time we'd run screaming in through it more than forty years earlier echoed in my memory. All packed up and gone now, it was the end of an era.

22

Phone Hacking

It was quite an eye-opener when I became aware of the extent of the symbiotic relationship between the police and the media. However, the releasing of information to the media in the case against Barry clearly emphasised the practice. The first time I understood that there was such an interdependent connection between the media and the police was when that first photograph of Barry was published. That picture, the one that caused the collapse of the first trial, could have come from no other source than the police. The photo was taken by them when Barry was arrested and after all of his belongings had been taken from him. Releasing that picture was a calculated strategy to make him look like a villain, and the media loved it. Forget 'innocent until proven guilty' when the media and the police collude with each other to use this type of propaganda against a defendant.

Speaking with reporters throughout the last number of years, I have found that both the police and journalists have a grudging need for this relationship. There's little love lost between them, but they rely on each other. It's easy to see the benefits of this type of cooperation, but there is far too much room for corruption. This can and does lead to justice being degraded. Evidence becomes a profitable commodity, and people's privacy is often sacrificed in order to gain some interesting piece of information in the race to be there at the conclusion of a case. This is what led to the phone-hacking scandal.

The hacking into the text messages on Millie Dowler's mobile phone seems to have led to the public exposure of this practice. It was highly insensitive, and pointed to the belief that Millie may actually still be alive for some time after she had been murdered. It was the highlighting of disgusting behaviour like this which eventually led to the closing of one particularly salacious Sunday newspaper, The News of the World, part of the Rupert Murdoch empire. Those of us who had suffered at the printing press of this publication's deceits breathed a huge sigh of relief when it finally closed for good.

This disgraceful conduct was also clearly evident in the reporting of the 2010 murder of landscape gardener Joanna Yates in Bristol. Joanna and her boyfriend lived in an apartment rented from landlord Mr Christopher Jefferies, a 65-year-old retired English teacher. It was Christmas, and the murder understandably attracted a lot of media attention. A pretty young student had been brutally murdered, and the press were baying for blood.

Watching a news programme, I saw Mr Jefferies talking to TV journalists outside of his home and the thought came to me, *Oh my goodness, he looks a bit suspicious* . . . Then I realised I had fallen into the media's trap. *No! Not you too, Michelle!* How could I have thought this way, after all we'd been through? Of all people, I had no right to prejudge someone because they were different nor to label someone as odd. Our family had suffered enough of that.

On the morning of December 30th 2010, Mr Jefferies was arrested at 7:00am for the murder of Joanna. He was taken into custody and kept for two days, then bailed. The ferocious media attack had started on the 29th of December, the day before his arrest. He was vilified and defamed, called a weirdo, loner, oddball, and more; all terms that were used against Barry. There was a complete character assassination of this well-spoken, intelligent and articulate man. The stories in the papers on December 30th recounting his arrest were written the night before, so as to be available to the public on the day. How did they know he was going to be arrested the night before his arrest?

Vincent Tabak, a neighbour, was charged on 22nd January 2011 with Joanna's murder, having confessed. Why was Mr Jefferies not released from bail until the 4th of March?

Christopher Jefferies case is a prime example of the police and the media forging a story together, having predetermined the outcome they wanted.

Jefferies, in an interview with the BBC, said, "As I had to hand over the clothes I was wearing and the possessions I had on me, it was as if the process of stripping me of my identity had begun." About the way he was treated by the police and in the media, he says, "It was a form of psychological torture."

Jefferies has since spoken at the Leveson Inquiry about the way he was treated by elements of the tabloid press. A two part docudrama was aired, starting on 10th December 2014 on ITV, called The Lost Honour of Christopher Jefferies.

In Barry's case, another misuse of this symbiotic relationship was the way the police used Nick Ross and the Crimewatch programme to propagate police agendas. Ross was close to Jill as they both co-hosted the Crimewatch programme for the BBC. Certainly Ross would have been profoundly affected by the awful murder of Jill. This was a shock to everyone, all journalists, celebrities and presenters, but Ross was the person who worked with Jill for four years on the show.

That a high profile celebrity could be ruthlessly murdered, and that the police had not brought anyone to justice, was bad enough. That the victim worked on a programme designed to help the police track down criminals made it so much worse; this crime seemed to be unsolvable. How could Jill Dando be killed in broad daylight, and the perpetrator evade detection? It was unthinkable. For the public, too, this undermined their confidence in the police and in the programme. How could one of their own not receive justice?

At the time of the murder, I recall thinking that with all the resources at their disposal, it would be a crime that would be solved quickly, but even with a reward offered of £250,000, no one had been found. Mansfield told me at the trial that celebrity and media confidence needed a conviction for this crime so that they could all feel safe again.

Regular viewers of Crimewatch might have seen the programme where the officer in charge of Operation Oxborough, Detective Chief Inspector Hamish Campbell, informed the public that the police were changing the focus of their investigation, and also the type of person they were seeking. Now, they were looking for a lone assassin, an obsessive, probably with an interest in guns, and with the ability to be in Fulham at that time. They asked the public for their help.

Worryingly, this public appeal was broadcasted just 24 hours after the police had finished their searches of Barry's flat on April 18th and 19th 2000. The police were asking the public to provide specific information to add to the circumstantial evidence they had already collected in their raids on his apartment, information which could help them to convict Barry George. Any evidence to the contrary, which might point to any other suspects, was not being sought. By narrowing down the focus of their investigation to just one possibility, they had effectively shut down any likelihood of finding other evidence. They had predetermined the outcome and had lost their objectivity.

When the police entered Barry's flat, they entered the chaotic world of a hoarder. Much was made of this disordered life by both the police and media; it was portrayed as somehow indicative of deviancy. The press loved this and duly printed every salacious photo they could find, which could only have come from the police during searches. Everything had been taken from the flat. The police even took swabs of the airbrick vents, and lifted floor-boards to seek evidence in the dust, but in this ramshackle apartment they could not detect a single particle of FDR, anywhere, and Barry didn't vacuum!

After the exposure of the hacking scandal, just about every celebrity, even those of minor stature and none, were found to have had their phones hacked. Barry's legal team asked the police for disclosure about their own phones, and ours. We were informed we were not among the thousands of people who'd had their messages and calls illegally intercepted. Not one journalist had wanted access to our communications . . . on one of the highest profile cases in British legal history! That is not credible. I've not heard whether Jill Dando's and Alan Farthing's phones were on that list either, but if they weren't, that would be inconceivable. We already know that journalists accessed Ms Dando's communications. Any news about her life was lucrative.

The reason this is so important is because the prosecution relied on something the police said in court: that no one knew Ms Dando was going to be at her home in Fulham on the day she was killed. Barry was supposed to have been hanging around in the street on the off-chance. In the light of this scandal, that has been blown out of the water. Journalists, and others, probably knew exactly where she would be.

So, what of Nick Ross – did he know something we all didn't? He seemed to think the police had kept him informed of things behind the scenes because of who he was, the presenter of Crimewatch. What incriminating evidence did they have that they didn't throw into the pot? This was a re-conviction they wanted very badly. What did they hold back?

Nothing . . . absolutely nothing. Everything they had they used, but they could not achieve a conviction this time. It's my belief that the police used Ross as part of their propaganda machine to undermine our efforts to obtain justice.

23

Falsely Accused and Non-disclosure

Being falsely accused of a sexual crime has been at the forefront of our news headlines recently. Liam Allan, a young man who had a consensual relationship with a woman for fourteen months, was under suspicion for raping the woman. He was arrested, then released on bail. If he had been convicted, he would have been on the sex offenders register and faced up to ten years in prison. He remained on bail for two years until, just one day before the trial was due to start, they received the evidence that had been withheld by the police because they said it wasn't relevant. Thousands of text messages from the accuser's mobile phone proved she was lying. Since then, many other cases have been exposed as fraudulent and have collapsed. Liam is backing a call for anonymity for rape suspects as well as for complainants.

In the wake of the shocking Jimmy Saville revelations, an appetite for witch hunting was born. Many public figures have been named as perpetrators of historic sex abuse and have lived under a cloud of suspicion with no way to prove their innocence. The police speak of "victims" and ask the public to come forward with more evidence against the accused. The accuser remains anonymous while the accused is exposed, named and shamed, and waits like a sitting duck for more accusations to be levelled.

Actors William Roache and Michael Lavelle were both found not guilty after their separate cases went to trial. Until they were exonerated they lived a nightmare existence, being vilified in the press. Their careers were at risk, as were their family lives. Even after being found not guilty, the press continued to write about them in accusatory tones. Politician's lives, especially dead ones who cannot fight back, have come under this sulphurous cloud of deceit. The smell sticks and they and their families can never be free from the corrosion of false accusations.

The so called investigation into the allegations of sexual misconduct against Sir Cliff Richard brought a new low to police/media conduct. Helicopters and TV cameras were on hand to witness the police entering his Berkshire apartment to carry out a search. Emblazoned all over the world were histrionic images, calculated to smear this celebrity entertainer. The world waited to see what fundamental piece of damning evidence was in the haul taken from the property. Nothing! Yet this man was exposed and vilified while the accuser remained unscathed. All allegations were dropped and Sir Cliff has won the cases taken out against South Yorkshire Police and the BBC.

Real abuse takes place far too regularly in real life. Those complainants need to know their cases will be taken seriously, but false accusers put these plaintiffs at risk of being tarred with the same brush. The public will start to believe they are all making up stories, our legal system will regress decades, and the factually abused will not feel safe in coming forward.

Police procedures must be reviewed, and the police and the CPS need to take responsibility for non-disclosure. Recently, Alison Saunders, Director of Public Prosecutions, was asked if innocent people could be in prison due to non-disclosure, she declared:

"I don't think so. The protections are there to make sure there is a fair trial and people are not wrongly imprisoned . . . If anyone thinks that there has been an issue, then they should be raising that and we can look at that again."

Alison Saunders must know this is nonsense. There are certainly innocents in jail and it is not as simple as just writing to Alison Saunders to ask her to review their cases. The long, drawn out appeals system insists on new evidence, often the very evidence that has been withheld.

There is a wealth of information still being withheld in the Jeremy Bamber case. Essex Police have refused to release documents and photos from the crime scene that were never shown to the jury. The courts have ordered them to release these documents but they still refuse, saying they are not relevant.

PII (Public Interest Immunity) has been used in many cases including that of Gerry Conlon, who asked for disclosure after his eventual release from prison. His records won't be available under PII until 2020. His family is still seeking that disclosure.

Gagging orders are another way the police and the justice system keep information under wraps. People are forbidden to disclose facts about their case, as happened to Eddie Gilfoyle, convicted of killing his pregnant wife in 1992. The police withheld evidence in his case which may have saved him from a wrongful conviction. Eddie, though freed in December 2010, was under a gagging order until January 2011, when the parole board concluded that its use of such an order was not lawful after they had been threatened that they would be challenged in the courts.

Throughout my involvement with victims of miscarriage of justice, I have met many people affected by non-disclosure and false allegations, but none so disturbing as the case of a man who addressed the 2007 INUK conference in Bristol and took the platform just before me on that day. A teacher, he'd been exonerated after the allegations of two young girls had been proven to be fallacious. His words, so softly spoken, will live with me for the rest of my life.

"When they found me guilty, I was in shock. How could this have happened? I was transferred to the prison and the guards processed me in. Then they led me to the section I was to be incarcerated in.

They had offered for me to go to the 'Nonce's' segregated area for my own protection, but I refused, because to go there was like admitting guilt, and I was innocent. So they took me to my section, opened the door where a group of inmates were gathered, then locked the door behind me. They were on the other side. I had been led like a sheep to slaughter. The crowd jumped me, they beat me up and stripped me naked. I was screaming "I'm innocent, I didn't do anything", but they wouldn't stop. The guards had known what was in store for me and had not stayed to help.

Then I saw the kettle . . . they held me down and poured boiling water over my genitals."

24

New Beginnings and Sad Farewells

Meeting and marrying Peter has been key to my new life, my new beginnings. Peter and I had been friends for a couple of years, but in 2012 we both realised we felt more than friendship for each other, a surprise to both of us because our lives were so different. Mine seemed to lurch from storm to hurricane with little respite. Peter's life was calm and ordered, though he was usually busy with family and with quiet ministry to others. How on earth could our lives come together? Surely they would collide and wipe each other out? But it wasn't Earth that was leading us to each other, it was God.

As Christians, obedient to Him, we stepped out in faith and He meshed our lives together. With God as the head of our marriage and with each of us putting the other's needs before our own, we have a union that is full of joy and laughter.

This life of gentle caring was foreign, and not what life had trained me for; it was a balm to my soul. For Peter, this merging certainly opened up areas of life that were outside of his previous experiences. Most of us like to cling to our comfort zones, our security blankets, but this is not God's way. My life had been catapulted out of anonymity in 2000 when Barry was arrested, and now Peter was shaken out of his because of his love for me. Many long-held beliefs were rattled and exposed as fraudulent when we came together:

Miscarriage of justice is rare – no it isn't.

Our justice system will always right its errors – no
it won't.

A person can't be found guilty if there is no evidence
they committed the crime – yes they can, they are.

You can't be convicted of a crime that never took
place – we know people who have been.

When Peter first met Barry he realised for himself how preposterous
was his conviction for this murder. The killing of Jill Dando has all
the hallmarks of a professional assassination, and Barry's chaotic
life disqualifies him as a candidate to carry out a perfect crime.

If meeting us had shaken Peter's life, he was about to be further
jarred. In Britain, there are two names synonymous with miscarriage
of justice: Paddy Hill and Gerry Conlon. Headliners; the complete
opposite of the safe, predictable, ordinary lives of most people. Peter
found himself moving in the previously unknown communities of
wrongful conviction, almost an underworld, separated from the
general populace. Having met Paddy and many other campaigners,
he was due to meet Gerry very soon.

Gerry had always had a soft spot for Barry, whom he knew to be
factually innocent. In 2011, Barry and I took a trip to Glasgow for
the 20th anniversary of the freeing of the Birmingham Six. We were
met at the train station by Cathy and Gerry and they immediately
wrapped us in huge hugs, then Barry and Gerry walked off to the
waiting cabs. Cathy hung back to talk to me.

"Michelle, Gerry shouldn't have come today. He needs emergency
dental treatment, he's in agony, but he wouldn't go until he'd greeted
Barry." I was truly touched by his compassion for Barry, someone
marginalised even before his wrongful conviction because of his
many disabilities.

It was the beginning of June 2014 when Cathy rang myself and
Peter, and I could tell she was upset and trying not to cry.

"Michelle, this is not public news, but Gerry asked me to tell his friends." Cathy told me that Gerry's illness was terminal. We'd known he was in hospital, but expected him to get well. My heart was heavy when I heard this news and I toyed with the idea of visiting Gerry in Belfast, but we couldn't go until he was out of hospital and back home. He thought he had a few weeks left.

I wrote to this dear, kind man. I couldn't bring myself to send a get well card; it would have been disingenuous. Gerry had been clear that he was dying, so I had to respect his honesty and meet it with the same. I shared from God's word. Words I felt both he and I could relate to: Psalm 27.

> The LORD is my light and my salvation –
>   whom shall I fear?
> The LORD is the stronghold of my life –
>   of whom shall I be afraid?
> When the wicked advance against me
>   to devour me,
> it is my enemies and my foes
>   who will stumble and fall.
> Though an army besiege me,
>   my heart will not fear;
> though war break out against me,
>   even then I will be confident.

Peter never did get to meet Gerry. Sadly, he died only a couple of weeks later on the 21st June. Barry came up from Cork to meet us in Belfast and attend the funeral. After a visit with Gerry's warm hearted family for the wake, Paul McLaughlin of MOJO accompanied us to a nearby pub to meet up with other mourners.

Peter had never been a frequenter of pubs and was not a drinker. We arrived at the public house to find that it had no windows and the doorway was not at the front. Once inside someone explained that, as the pub was often fired at in drive-by shootings during the troubles, it was safer to block off the windows and to offset the entrance for security purposes. For an English man, being in this setting was a bizarre experience. Peter was standing in a pub on the Falls Road in Belfast!

Suddenly Peter found himself wrapped in a powerful hug. It was Paddy Hill, and he was sobbing his heart out on Peter's shoulder, pouring out his grief at the loss of his friend.

Oh, what changes were wrought in your life, darling Perter, when you decided to make me your wife, your . . . trouble and strife.

The funeral was held in St Peter's Cathedral in Belfast and the celebrant, Father Ciaran Dallat, talked of his concerns for Gerry's eternal life.

"I wanted to talk about his salvation, but when I visited with Gerry he told me . . . *I know Jesus is my saviour.* Gerry was at peace and prepared to meet God and be reunited with his parents again, in Heaven."

Looking around the gathering of family and friends, believers and non-believers, a diverse group that included many miscarriage of justice survivors, I could see I was not the only one sobbing, but mine were tears of pure joy.

25

Ripple Effect

Drop a pebble in the water; just a splash, and it is gone;
But there's half-a-hundred ripples circling on and on
and on,
Spreading, spreading from the centre, flowing on out to
the sea.
And there is no way of telling where the end is going
to be.

"A Lesson From a Pebble" – James W. Foley

When a miscarriage of justice occurs, the fallout from it will be far reaching. Take, for example, three well known miscarriage of justice cases: The Birmingham Six, The Guildford Four and The Maguire Seven. Seventeen people wrongfully convicted, seventeen lives wounded beyond repair, but the reality is much, much worse. For each wrongly convicted person, there is a ripple effect of damage.

In the immediate aftermath of a wrongful conviction it feels as though the world has been turned upside down. Wrongly convict one person, and the consequences are that there will be a detrimental effect on the lives of their parents, their spouse, children, relatives, friends, work colleagues, neighbours and more. The burden for bringing up a family now falls completely to the other spouse, and the loss of wages leads to rent or mortgages becoming too high a load to bear.

Children have to learn to live without the support of one parent, and relationships often break down, sometimes irreparably. Paddy Hill lost everything: he could not support his wife and young family from a cell, and it became just too hard for them to keep up with his constantly being moved from prison to prison. His wife would arrive for a visit with all the children in tow, only to be told he'd been moved to another place further away. The term for this is 'ghosting'. This was their punishment for being related to a person convicted of a heinous crime. Relationships eventually broke down and the marriage ended. Some bonds Paddy managed to rebuild after he was released, but others could not be resurrected.

My dear friend Gerry Conlon lost not only his liberty, but his father too. Giuseppe Conlon died in prison for a crime neither he nor his son had committed. Giuseppe heard of his son's arrest and travelled to Britain to try to sort out the mistake; his only crime was his concern for his son. Gerry's Mum, travelling from Belfast to visit them both, experienced the same terrible ordeal with prison visits as the others did: they'd been moved!

All families of the wrongly convicted become prisoners as well. Life becomes a round of visits, battles and struggles just to keep going. It's hard for those whose loved ones are in jail as a consequence of their own actions, but if they shouldn't be there at all, it is all the more painful.

Back home in Cork, we experienced this ripple effect. Neighbours of ours had to put up with journalists turning up on their doorsteps seeking dirt on us. There was nothing to smear us with, but they still kept ringing doorbells, asking for information or photos of Barry, even though Barry had not been to Cork since 1982 and nobody knew him. One young woman didn't even live in Ballincollig anymore: she had moved to Paris for work. She vaguely knew of me, but knew nothing at all of Barry or this case. Somehow journalists in Paris found out her family lived locally to mine . . . she was tracked down by the media and then harassed in the streets, followed and shouted at, left fearful for her safety. In Paris, for goodness sake!

Many of our more distant relatives were tracked down and offered money for stories or photos. These were people just living their own lives, nothing to do with the death of Jill Dando. Fortunately, my Limerick relatives are wonderful people of integrity. Otherwise, I hate to think what sort of reception those annoying young whippersnapper journalists might have encountered.

Mum, of course, had the breakdown from which she never fully recovered. My 70-year-old Dad was attacked and knocked to the ground in Wales, where he lived, because he told a lout who was haranguing him that his son was innocent. The emotional effect on me and on my family is evident. Also, Mike, Mum and myself are well out of pocket and will never be recompensed.

Mrs Susan Bicknell first set eyes on Barry at 11:50am on 26th April 1999. Mrs Bicknell knew he had been there for up to twenty-minutes, waiting, because first he had to gain admittance. Then he had to be spoken to by Rosario Torres, and then, when he persisted in being seen *today*, his presence had been escalated to the manager, Lesley.

During the trial in 2001, Mrs Bicknell found herself the butt of nasty innuendos by the police and the prosecution. She was unwell, but had chosen to come to court anyway. Comments like, 'She's as sick as those she's working with' were made, because she was suffering from a mental health illness brought on by the extreme stress she was under. At the time of the encounter with Barry, Mrs Bicknell had been married for just six weeks. She lost her job through ill-health, they lost their home because they could not pay the mortgage, and the media decided to vilify this innocent woman just because she had the temerity to say Barry was at HAFAD between 11:30 and 12:00 on April 26th.

Mrs Bicknell travelled to the Old Bailey for the retrial, too, and waited to be called to give evidence once again. She was not called, and she was never told why. She also didn't know that the other HAFAD witnesses had all revised their times, realising they had made errors, and that they now coincided with hers. Basically,

Mrs Bicknell was not considered a credible witness due to her breakdown, caused by the stress of being a witness.

Throughout these years I've been lauded for all the work I did on Barry's behalf, culminating in his eventual release. People have said things like, 'Where would he have been without you?' and, 'Aren't you wonderful to do what you did?' These well-intentioned comments have always made me feel distinctly uncomfortable, because I really didn't do much at all. Yes, there were sacrifices, there was a financial drain and huge stress, but this was my brother. He'd been badly wronged and needed help. All I did was what God asked me to do: *stand!* Many people did far more than I ever could: MOJO volunteers, various legal counsel, medical professionals, journalists and a myriad of other people that God sent in. I can claim no kudos.

One unsung hero is Mike. Although we didn't always see eye to eye on how to campaign to best effect (who knew, anyway?), he was a constant supporter to my mum and a stalwart campaigner for Barry. Family relationships were unstable during this time to say the least, but Mike kept on visiting Barry in prison, staying with Mum, and was an avid writer of letters, both to Barry and on his behalf to anyone who may be able to help us.

It was Mike who set up the 'Justice for Barry' website and ran it with help from investigative journalist and author, Scott Lomax. I was personally very grateful for this, because I'd been feeling guilty for not doing it myself as Barry was constantly asking me to. It helped that Mike didn't have children and homework waiting for him when he got home from work, but he could have just sat back and done nothing. There were others, within and outside of the family who couldn't offer to help, for whatever reason. Basically, it was Mum, myself and Mike as the three planks of immediate support for Barry at this time. For the most part, people didn't want to run the gauntlet of media intrusion into their lives, and I, for one, couldn't blame them for that.

Two of my cousins were in this situation, but they'd both contacted me right at the beginning to say they believed Barry was innocent. We three met up in a local wine bar in Hammersmith Broadway for a catch-up and giggles over glasses of rosé from time to time. This was a lifeline for me, and really helped me cope with the loneliness of being away from home and the stress of the battles we were facing.

The sad truth is that most people will run for cover because the media can be relentless in their trawl for the next storyline. Truth and justice are sacrificed to the need to keep huge numbers of people in jobs at various news groups.

In one of my late night phone conversations with Hazel Keirle, while organising the appeal, she also said I was good to be so supportive of Barry.

"No, not really, Hazel," I replied. "I didn't have a choice. It has to be done and Mum can't do it."

"No, Michelle," came Hazel's forceful reply. "You had a choice and you made it! There are many victims of miscarriage of justice who find themselves completely on their own in this nightmare. Often family and friends believe they *must* be guilty if the courts have convicted them, and they don't want to be tarred with the same brush."

Goodness, I had never realised that family might not step up to the mark to help a wrongly convicted person. If anyone I knew was in prison for a crime committed by someone else, I'd have to try to help . . . I believed all families would. Sadly, Mum, Mike and I were to find out that you battle against this giant alone. Disagreements aside, we were the three Musketeers.

At times, Mum could make life very uncomfortable when Mike stayed with her, but he knew how much she needed his support to keep going. She could be short-tempered and hurtful with me, too. Her irascible moods and snappy comments were tough to endure, but they came from a place of pain, and so we bore with her. That is, until the day came I could take no more and I threatened to go back home to Cork.

"Mum, I'm sorry but I've had enough. I'm not taking any more of this attitude from you. This is *your* son I'm supporting, not mine. My son is back in Cork with his two sisters, all missing their Mum. Either this sniping ends or I go back home, and since I can't afford to pay for hotel accommodation when I come over, if I can't stay here, I can't continue to do what I'm doing for Barry. You decide!"

It really takes an awful lot to make me confrontational. I hate it, but I had to make Mum realise that she was in danger of alienating the very people who were working for Barry. We knew why she was doing this – she wished for it all to go away – but the only thing going away would have been us. After my outburst she was calmer towards us all, though we could still see how hard it was for her to have people in the home that she usually had to herself.

Mike was unwavering in his support of Barry, and was often quoted in newspapers, both in the UK and in Ireland, leading to some people who were upset by this telling him to pack it in . . . 'Can't you just put your head down and keep quiet?' Like me, he could not do that while Barry languished in prison for murder. Having assessed the paucity of evidence for himself, Mike had gone out of his way to help: he has an innate sense of justice. Also, I believe he'd have been there for Barry even if he had been the killer, but he would *never* have campaigned for his freedom.

The following are the poignant and personal thoughts of my younger children. Their words sum up what it felt like for them growing up with the fear, the confusion and the crippling sense of injustice as we battled for years for their uncle's freedom.

Shane's Story

My uncle Barry had always lived in London and so I didn't really know him. I had photos of him, of course, but not really memories. When everything started in 2000 I was thirteen and I don't remember very much about it, except being sent to stay with my friend at his house. Mum was away a lot because she was helping

Barry and staying with Nana, and we couldn't be at home alone when Dad went to work. I didn't mind too much because I got to have fun with my friends, going fishing or hill walking. I did miss my own home, though. I also missed my Mum. It was rather strange seeing her on the news or being interviewed in a newspaper. Everyone in Ballincollig knew that was my Mum on TV, and my friends would often talk to me about Barry being locked up, but it was never negative. No one ever made me feel bad because of it. People were upset for us and for Barry because he shouldn't have been in prison. I felt quite proud of my Mum for standing up for her brother, it was very hard on her.

Later, after Barry came to Cork to live, I moved into his apartment with him for a few months. It was great spending time with him and I quite enjoyed cooking meals and keeping the apartment organised. I know Barry was very grateful for this help, too, but eventually he asked me to move out because it was too difficult for him to live with someone else. I couldn't understand what I'd done, or why he felt so anxious, but Mum explained it was a reaction to all that had happened to him. It does make me so mad to think that my uncle had to go through eight years in prison when it was obvious he wasn't guilty. He's been very badly affected by it, and I'm not sure he can ever fully recover. Being told he's not innocent enough after all of this is just so unfair.

Emma's Experiences

When all of this started in 2000, I was only ten years old, the youngest in the family. I don't remember many details, but it was a confusing time, and I really missed my Mum when she left to go to England. One thing I do remember is how hard it was to answer the questions of my friends. I never knew if I would say something the wrong way, or get it all wrong. Sometimes I was sent to stay with my friend's parents and it made me very upset. Even though they were really good to me, I just wanted to be in my own home, to be with my brother and sister, and to sleep in my own bed. We also had lots of pets and I missed them, too.

Dad never spoke about what was happening in England with the trial and everything, but one day we came into the front room to find him sobbing. He had tears running down his face. We were terrified; we didn't know what could have caused this. I had never seen my Dad cry before. Then he told us. He kept saying, "He's been convicted, he's been convicted." He was inconsolable.

I was in secondary school when Barry won his appeal, but it was overshadowed because we'd lost our Dad a few months earlier. Mum offered to stay home with us, but we three had already discussed this and told her to go and help Barry. We had each other; he had no one. In one way I meant it, but in another I didn't. I was always worried when she was away.

When we heard the news that my uncle had been found not guilty, I rang my Mum in England. We were all cheering and crying at home. Later that year, I had to go to hospital. Thank goodness Mum was back from England. She had Barry with her and it was great to finally see him. Mum took me to A&E and the doctor said I needed emergency surgery. I was taken down next morning.

When I came around, my loved ones were all standing by my bedside: my husband-to-be Denis, my Mum, Barry, my brother Shane and a friend. Barry gave me a big bag from Boots, the chemist. It had a pink wash-bag and pretty smelling things for my hospital stay. He was so sweet.

The next day, I caught sight of a newspaper on another patient's table. The headline was horrible, and there was a photo of my visitors leaving the hospital in the rain. It said my Mum had taken Barry to the mental ward! I was terribly upset, and even though everyone tried to tell me it wasn't my fault, I felt guilty. If I hadn't been in hospital, my uncle wouldn't have been photographed in the street. Another paper had a photo of Barry carrying the Boots bag as he came out of the chemist shop in Patrick Street. It was all so unfair.

One day, my best friend Ann and I met up after college. She really wanted to tell me about what happened that day.

"Our group were asked to think about a strong woman, someone we admire, then tell the group why. Most people talked about celebrities or famous women from history, like Anne Frank, or the first female president of Ireland, Mary Robinson. When it was my turn to share, I said Michelle Diskin. No one knew who I was talking about, so I told them how your Mum is so strong and courageous, what she did for Barry and how she really inspires me."

I had never felt so pleased in all my life! My Mum was special to me, but I never thought about how other people saw her. She was like a famous person. It was definitely my proudest moment.

Now having become a Mum myself, I can see how hard it must have been for her to go away and leave her children behind. She must have been in bits. I couldn't bear to leave my gorgeous son and travel away. I am so proud of my Mum. She inspires me, too.

26

Healing and Moving On

The healing of damaged relationships is difficult to achieve after a miscarriage of justice. People have been hurt; words have been spoken that cannot be taken back. Trust will have broken down, and bitterness can become the driving force in many lives.

Guilt, anger, fear, denial, pain, confusion and blame. These are all emotions I have either experienced or witnessed since Barry's release. When a loved one is incarcerated unjustly, these forces first come into play in relational dynamics. During the ensuing battles, any one of those forces can rise to the surface and predominate, changing as the wind blows.

This gamut of emotions rises again after the initial, endorphin-fuelled high of the release. There will be PTSD to deal with for the acquitted, and families are not equipped to deal with this destructive condition. Barry and I clashed many times, with me being the one to shout and scream at the poor guy for his unintentionally injurious effect on our family's life. I shouted, stormed and blazed. Barry looked on, confusion in his eyes, speaking words of apology to me. He didn't mean to be difficult and couldn't understand my volatility. His disabilities and his PTSD, along with my swamped emotional state, created an explosive mix.

Outside of just we two, there were others who were feeling many of these emotions as well. None of us had a magic wand to wave that would make all of this disappear. We needed to find a way to straddle this new hurdle in our lives or we'd sink under the pressure.

Forgiveness was what we needed, and peace and calmness. Salve for our battered souls. Each one needed to forgive themselves, first for the 'shoulda, woulda, coulda' feelings of the past. These self-recriminations serve no purpose other than to burden each of us with guilt. Forgiveness, too, for those we perceived had trespassed against us. Holding grudges doesn't make us feel better or bring about restitution. The trespasser may not even know they've hurt us, or care. The forgiveness here is not to let the offender off the hook, but to set ourselves free from their bondage.

A lack of forgiveness troubles the soul, like writhing worms, eating us up from the inside and filling the soul with bitterness. God knows that forgiveness is for us, and it does not include forgetting – that could prove impossible, or just plain dangerous. It also doesn't mean that a person has been forgiven by God, they will have to go to Him themselves to ask for His absolution.

Barry could have chosen to live in a world full of recrimination and bitterness, but he decided that this appalling wrong had taken enough from his life, and that he would not give the police or the justice system any more power to hurt him. When asked by the BBC in February 2015 about those who wronged him, he said, "I forgive, but I don't forget."

It has been ten years since Barry's release in 2008, and it is good to see relationships starting to be renewed. Old hurts are being mended, new respect being forged. Each one is seeking to leave the damage behind them and rise from the ashes of the past. Souls are emerging from stasis as old wounds grow new skin.

It would be so encouraging to be able to say that all of our woes are over, that we are now free and Barry has been able to return to the country of his birth to start life afresh. Sadly, this is not so. Barry is still in exile. If he came back to the UK, he would have to live in temporary accommodation again, which is far from ideal. Of course, Barry is not the only released non-offender to find himself in this unenviable position. Speaking with other released wrongly convicted showed me that this government is not exercising its duty of care to these citizens. Paul and Cathy at the MOJO offices in

Glasgow have been outlining new initiatives to highlight the plight of their released clients. Barry and I have agreed to do whatever we can to assist and support them in this endeavour. We have also been working closely with Mark Williams Thomas, investigative journalist, who has shown a keen interest in seeing this case solved.

History shows that we must stand up for justice wherever injustice is found. Women in Britain would still not have a say in our society if the Suffragettes and Suffragists had not fought and lobbied, long and hard, for votes for women. Now we look down on other countries and cultures and condemn them for their discriminatory behaviour, and rightly so, but we do this while forgetting that society here once tried to keep women in subjugation by all means available to it. Women's right were hard won. The same can be said of workers' rights, and of gender and racial inequality. The fight for justice must go on.

Barry and I are held up as victors and survivors of miscarriage of justice amongst other families in the same position, who take heart from our victory. That's why I'm often asked if I have any advice for other families who are going through this nightmare. Of course, I don't have the monopoly on wisdom, but if anything I say helps just one family then it is worth passing it on.

My first piece of advice is aimed at families who have not actually suffered a wrongful conviction yet, but whose loved one is in custody for something they didn't do. They need to ensure the defendant has their own legal representation. I know this can be hard to do in these times of severe cuts to legal aid, but it is vitally important. A solicitor is not allowed to do anything that might damage their client's defence. If, as in joint enterprise cases, there are guilty and innocent in a group, the solicitor will not be able to go against the perpetrators to seek justice for the factually innocent. Most families are not aware of this, and blithely trust in a single duty-solicitor for the group, believing their rights are being safeguarded.

My second piece of guidance would have to be: *do not fight unless there is something to be gained*. This is tantamount to banging your head against a brick wall, and will ensure you are worn out all of the time. Remember, you are not to blame for what has happened to your loved one, and you are doing all that you can to put it right. There will be enough real battles to fight, don't waste energy fighting to no purpose.

Remember, too, the media are not there to highlight your plight. Their agenda is likely to differ from yours as we found out to our cost with the News of the World. The press' loyalty is first to their revenue, and then to their readership, not to you. I used some very specific strategies when navigating my way through this media minefield that I feel worked for me. I never, never allowed them to see my real emotions, whether sad or just plain angry, no swearing, no shouting. Although funds were short I always appeared dressed for business, there is much more value in a photo of a person in baggy leggings and with unkempt hair. Whatever the family's circumstances, remain steadfastly dignified, because this does not sell newspapers.

Be wise if working with the press or TV when trying to show your loved one's innocence. The Hillsborough football stadium disaster in 1989, when ninety-six Liverpool football fans lost their lives, and the subsequent defamation of these innocent fans by a news publication, is a perfect example of why you must be diligent.

And lastly, try not to neglect other family members, they will need your time, too, especially if there are little ones. Set aside some time to go on days out – a picnic in the park, a visit to a museum. There are many enjoyable activities that don't cost much money or can even be enjoyed for free. It is by doing these things, and not getting sucked into a guilt trip of frenetic activity, that the family stands a chance of still being intact when the eventual release comes.

"Injustice anywhere is a threat to justice everywhere."
Martin Luther King Jr.

27

Epilogue

"Look back in forgiveness, forward with hope, down in compassion and up with gratitude."

Zig Ziglar

Time marches on.

It has now been eighteen years since that radio broadcast on RTÉ that changed my life. Today, my life looks very different to the one I was living in May 2000. I have watched as my three lovely children have made the transition from childhood into the world as adults. I am so proud of them and how they have grown into totally unselfish, responsible and fun-loving people. Each of them has battled adversity; nothing has come easily. Each has a compassion for others, and an ability to stand up and say 'No!' when things need challenging. They do not suffer fools gladly, nor accept injustice. The life lessons of adversity have taught them well. They didn't have a choice about whether they would face such traumas, but they had a choice about how they would respond to them. They chose not sink below, but to rise above.

Losing their Dad in the midst of all of this was extraordinarily painful for them, and they found it difficult to come to me with their grief, always trying not to add to my pressure. I am so grateful for their wonderfully supportive friends who came alongside and walked this sorrowful path with them. You are my honorary children, and I love you all to bits. I am so proud of *you*, too.

While it has been rewarding to rekindle relationships, returning to other aspects of my life has been personally enriching. I am excited to think about starting up a part-time consultancy next year, using my training as an Image and Style Consultant. My dreams have lain dormant for most of these years – The Barry Years, as I now think of them. I've always enjoyed seeing how empowering it is to others to know themselves better; it builds self-esteem and confidence, and it is the most personally fulfilling profession to be in for me.

Peter and I married in 2012, on the wettest day of the wettest November since records began. I didn't care. I had my home grown bridesmaids, my two beautiful girls, and my handsome son to escort me down the aisle. Best of all, I had a wonderful man by my side. Could I have been more blessed?

We have grown together well. Peter provides a harmonious environment for me to grow in and a place of refuge when I need it. My joy has been multiplied by the growing love between my lovely husband for his step-children, and their love and acceptance of the man I love. We've been further blessed by the arrival of Emma and Denis's first born in 2016: Tommy, our treasured grandson.

Peter and I are now undertaking new adventures together. Involvement with church is ongoing, and we are also advocates of many charities in the UK and other places such as The Gambia, Uganda, and Kosovo. In 2002, Peter had heard God's voice within him say: *"If you love me, you will go."* He did. He went to Kosovo after the war of 1999, and has seen many miracles happen in the lives of these war-torn people and the rebuilding of their society. We both know many wonderful people through the continuation of this work. It was also through this work that I met another man, who had also answered the call to go. Robin Croxon heard my story from Peter and, believing in it, set me on the road to having this book published. With his background in publishing, he knew all the right people.

Currently, I am enjoying life in a pretty little village in Northamptonshire, and hoping to find more time for family life, travel and for fun! Of course, it won't be possible for any of us to put all of this completely behind us. There is still more work to be done. I have become a patron of UAI and continue to attend meetings and speak at various venues about miscarriages of justice. Also, as a patron of JB Campaign Ltd, an organisation run by academics and professionals campaigning for justice for Jeremy Bamber, I am in good company. Judges, barristers, human rights campaigners, a former MP, celebrities, authors and others who were wrongly convicted make up the patronage who support this demand for justice.

Barry is still seeking redress from the government for his wrongful conviction, and supports those who are trying to overturn the unworkable law that sees the defendant being asked to 'prove their innocence beyond reasonable doubt' when there is no judicial mechanism by which to do this. He has always felt an obligation to use his suffering to help those still battling for freedom, knowing they may face the same injustices when released.

It's important that I clearly state this: our family do not see the police as our enemies. We need our brave men and women. They have a difficult job to do, and often put their very lives at risk to keep us safe. All of the officers I know are good people who entered the force to do the right thing: to serve justice. Obviously, there are deep concerns over policing methods and these need to be addressed, urgently. Withholding evidence or cherry-picking evidence seems to be endemic in the force and it is not acceptable. These practices must be eradicated. The rules and guidelines are there already, they just need to be enforced.

But what about Jill Dando? Her case is still in an 'unsolved' file, gathering dust in a Met Police facility. Her family still don't know who killed her, or why. They need answers. Jill's memory deserves to be honoured, and this case needs to be reinvestigated, looking at all of the other unused evidence. The Met Police response to queries about the case is that "the case is still open, and any new evidence will be examined".

I believe it is time for another police force to review this case. Maybe not being under the same pressure to be seen to get a conviction, or in the glare of the media, their unbiased appraisal may well uncover the proof needed to bring the real killer to trial.

Both Jill and Barry may, at long last, receive the justice they deserve.

Author's Notes

This book has been written from my perspective and from my memory. Of course, I do understand that other's recollections may differ from mine; that is the nature of memory, it is not infallible. Also, I do ask for forgiveness if anyone feels I missed their name out of the book. I have not intentionally left you out, there was just a limit to how much I could record of the past twenty years in one book. Therefore, not every incident or person appears in these pages. To do that would have necessitated a hefty tome. Barry decided not to add a chapter to the book. Obviously, his experiences from inside prison would be very different from ours on the outside, and he'd like to document this in his own words.

Writing about our family's experiences has been a very difficult experience for me. Each instance was relived in vivid colour, with the same intense pain it carried at the time. Sadly, there are very many families going through this torment, even as I write, and many have, and are, experiencing a far more torturous time than we ever did. My heart goes out to them. The high profile of the victim in Barry's case may have led to his wrongful conviction, but it also helped his case to remain in the public arena. Most victims of wrongful conviction are easily forgotten.

Wrongful accusations and convictions cause acute life altering anguish. Society needs to understand the torment of these families, and try to support them through their trauma. If our family's experience had been unusual I would probably not have felt the need to record it in a book. I would have done what most do, put my head down and tried to get on with my own life. Regrettably, instances of wrongful conviction are far from uncommon. The public may hear from the victim, but rarely the ripple effect on family and friends.

It is my sincere hope that those who read this story will see our shattered lives as more than just a sound bite or a two minute news item. I pray that they will see the lives behind the exposition.

In Christ alone my hope is found

In Christ alone my hope is found,
He is my light, my strength, my song;
This Cornerstone, this solid Ground,
Firm through the fiercest drought and storm.
What heights of love, what depths of peace,
When fears are stilled, when strivings cease!
My Comforter, my All in All,
Here in the love of Christ I stand.

In Christ alone! – who took on flesh,
Fullness of God in helpless babe.
This gift of love and righteousness,
Scorned by the ones He came to save:
Till on that cross as Jesus died,
The wrath of God was satisfied –
For every sin on Him was laid;
Here in the death of Christ I live.

There in the ground His body lay,
Light of the world by darkness slain:
Then bursting forth in glorious day
Up from the grave He rose again!
And as He stands in victory
Sin's curse has lost its grip on me,
For I am His and He is mine –
Bought with the precious blood of Christ.

No guilt in life, no fear in death,
This is the power of Christ in me;
From life's first cry to final breath,
Jesus commands my destiny.
No power of hell, no scheme of man,
Can ever pluck me from His hand:
Till He returns or calls me home,
Here in the power of Christ I'll stand.

Publications

Burke, Mike:

The Battle to Clear Barry George of the Jill Dando murder.

Hill, Paddy Joe:

Forever Lost, Forever Gone.

Lomax, Scott:

The Case of Barry George.
Who Killed Jill Dando?: The Case of Barry George, A Shocking Miscarriage of Justice.

Justice for Jill: How the Wrong Man was Jailed for the Murder of Jill Dando.

Jeremy Bamber.

Naughton, Michael:

The Innocent and the Criminal Justice System: A Sociological Analysis of Miscarriages of Justice.

The Criminal Cases Review Commission: Hope for the Innocent.

Support Organisations to contact
for more assistance:

Miscarriages of Justice Organisation

An Independent Human Rights Organisation Providing Support
& Assistance to Victims of Miscarriage Of Justice

What is MOJO? The Miscarriages of Justice Organisation
(MOJO) is a not-for-profit human rights organisation, set up by
Paddy Hill and John McManus in 2001. As an organisation we
are dedicated to assisting innocent people, both in prison and on
release, and their families. Our objective is to meet the whole needs
of the miscarriage of justice victim, from wrongful conviction,
through release, to compensation and beyond. We bring under one
roof the legal, medical and everyday support needs of our clients
whilst campaigning on all issues relating to miscarriage of justice

What We Do . . .

Legal – Our legal team of qualified and student lawyers assists
in the formulation and pursuit of criminal appeals. We fill a gap in
provision created by the lack of resources available to the majority
of those seeking to appeal their conviction. (This service is currently
available only in Scotland)

Aftercare – Our drop-in service, available 5 days per week –
aims to meet the ongoing needs of liberated miscarriage of justice
victims, whether exonerated or seeking to overturn convictions
after completion of sentence. We address their practical daily needs
– health, housing, benefits – as well as providing emotional support
to assist in their reintegration to our communities.

Campaigning – We campaign on all issues related to miscarriage of justice. We seek reform of the criminal justice system, and fight for the establishment of better, broader and more accessible services for miscarriage of justice victims and their families. We support individual, case-specific, campaigns and also wider movements seeking much-needed change in the approach to miscarriage of justice, and its effects. For most of our clients we are the last hope. Wrongful conviction and imprisonment effects not only the wrongly accused; it impacts hugely on their family and friends, who become secondary victims. It really could be you next

Support, Donate & Raise Funds – We rely heavily on affiliation fees and donations, now more than ever. Our workload is increasing – we currently receive over 200 requests for assistance per year, and this number is rising. Without your support we simply cannot function. Now more than ever it is crucial that MOJO continues its work. Your support will enable us to continue visiting the innocent in prison, build our pro bono legal team facilitate access to educational courses and social activities, like outward-bound courses, music, art and drama therapy, to aid in the rehabilitation and reintegration of miscarriage of justice victims. It will allow us to meet immediate needs by supplying care packages of bedding, clothing and food. Your support will allow us to campaign for the change we need.

Please donate, either by sending us a cheque or through PayPal at
https://paypal.me/mojopay
121-127 Saltmarket, Glasgow, G1 5LF
Tel: 0141 552 0009
info@miscarriagesofjustice.org
www.miscarriagesofjustice.org

Registered Charity No. SC033820

UNITED AGAINST INJUSTICE

United Against Injustice

Kevin McMahon formed Merseyside Against Injustice in 1998, he helped and encouraged the formation of other groups all over the UK, London Against Injustice, Kent Against Injustice, Yorkshire and Humberside Against Injustice etc. The choice of name was on purpose to unify these groups while they acted entirely independently. In 2001 Kevin founded United Against Injustice (UAI) to federate and bring these and other groups together while they remained independent groups.

Over the years United Against Injustice has adapted its working structure. It is run by family members and supporters of people who have been wrongly convicted of serious crimes and is hosted by Liverpool John Moores University with the help of their long-time supporters Prof Joe Sim and Anne Hayes from the University. Joe Sim chaired the very first meeting of UAI at the CASA where UAI hold their networking and social evening after the conference.

The organisers are volunteers, they are not paid and have never received any expenses. They now enjoy the patronage of Michelle Diskin-Bates and the actor Dean Sullivan and cherish the support they receive from many others. UAI consider themselves as a family and do not underestimate the importance of UAI as a support organisation.

Every year UAI holds a day conference of workshops followed by a meeting with national and international speakers of prominence many of which are world experts in their field. UAI does not take on case work.

UAI provides a platform for speakers to tell about their individual cases and campaigns, these are often heart-breaking stories and sharply illustrate the extent and gravity of the problem.

The Conference is always free and open to everyone interested in understanding and campaigning about miscarriages of justice. UAI conferences are exceptional in the UK for providing networking and access to experts which ordinarily would be difficult to contact. In 2018 UAI are holding their 17th Annual Conference

What cannot be described is the impact UAI conferences have on individuals and their cases their feedback often credits attending the conference as the real breakthrough with their case.

UAI can be contacted at:

http://www.unitedagainstinjustice.com
email: contact@unitedagainstinjustice.com
http://facebook.com/groups/487090761485587/